DISCOVERING
VINTAGE
Philadelphia

DISCOVERING
VINTAGE
Philadelphia

A Guide to the City's Timeless
Shops, Bars, Delis & More

TANYA BIRCH

Globe
Pequot

Guilford, Connecticut

All the information in this guidebook is subject to change. We recommend that you call ahead to obtain current information before traveling.

Globe Pequot

An imprint of Rowman & Littlefield

Distributed by NATIONAL BOOK NETWORK

The Discovering Vintage series was created by Mitch Broder, the author of *Discovering Vintage New York: A Guide to the City's Timeless Shops, Bars, Delis & More.*

British Library Cataloguing in Publication Information Available

Library of Congress Cataloging-in-Publication Data

Birch, Tanya.
  Discovering vintage Philadelphia : a guide to the city's timeless shops, bars, delis & more / Tanya Birch. — First edition.
    pages cm
  Includes bibliographical references and index.
  ISBN 978-1-4930-1261-9 (paperback : alkaline paper) — ISBN 978-1-4930-1400-2 (e-book) 1. Philadelphia (Pa.)—Guidebooks. 2. Stores, Retail—Pennsylvania—Philadelphia—Guidebooks. 3. Delicatessens—Pennsylvania—Philadelphia—Guidebooks. 4. Bars (Drinking establishments)—Pennsylvania—Philadelphia—Guidebooks. 5. Restaurants—Pennsylvania—Philadelphia—Guidebooks. 6. Historic buildings—Pennsylvania—Philadelphia—Guidebooks. I. Title.
  F158.18.B57 2015
  974.8'11—dc23
                                                    2015005608

This book is dedicated in memory of
Mary Caffas, a devoted, caring teacher in the small town
where I grew up, who always encouraged me to keep writing.

Contents

Introduction xv

Bassetts Ice Cream 1

Bob & Barbara's Lounge 5

Bomb Bomb BBQ Grill & Italian Restaurant 9

Cacia's Bakery 13

Campo's Deli 17

Cappuccio's Meats 20

Cherry Street Tavern 25

City Tavern Restaurant 29

Cookie's Tavern 33

Cosmi's Deli 37

Cunningham Piano Company 41

Czerw's Polish Kielbasa 45

Dalessandro's Steaks and Hoagies 49

DeLuca's Villa di Roma 53

Di Bruno Bros. 56

The Dining Car 60

Dirty Frank's Bar 65

Esposito's Meats 69

Famous 4th Street Delicatessen 72

Fante's Kitchen Shop 76

Fleishman Fabrics & Supplies 79

Frederick W. Oster Fine Violins & Vintage Instruments . . 82

Geno's Steaks 87

Goldstein's Men's and Boys' Clothing 91

Humphrys Flag Company 95

Iannelli's Bakery 99

Isgro Pasticceria 103

Joe's Steaks & Soda Shop 108

John's Roast Pork 111

John's Water Ice 115

Joseph Fox Bookshop 118

Lucio Mancuso & Son 122

McGillin's Olde Ale House 125

McMenamin's Tavern 129

McNally's Tavern 133

The Mermaid Inn 136

Old Original Nick's Roast Beef 139

P&F Giordano 143

Pat's King of Steaks 147

Pop's Water Ice 151

Ralph's Italian Restaurant 155

Ray's Happy Birthday Bar 159

Sarcone's Bakery 162

Shane Confectionary 165

Smokey Joe's 169

Snockey's Oyster and Crab House 173

Stock's Bakery. 177

Superior Pasta Company. 180

Swiacki Meats 184

The Victor Café 188

Other Vintage Spots around Philadelphia

McGlinchey's Bar 7

Fiorella's Sausage. 23

Cannuli's Quality Meats & Poultry. 23

Jim's Steaks 51

DiNic's Pork & Beef 52

Claudio Specialty Foods 58

Melrose Diner 62

Mayfair Diner 62

Halloween 67

Koch's Deli. 75

Freeman's Auction House 85

Mitchell & Ness Nostalgia Company 93

Marra's of Philadelphia 101

Tacconelli's Pizzeria. 101

Termini Brothers Bakery 106

Giovanni's Room 120

Grey Lodge Pub. 131

Dante & Luigi's, Corona di Ferro. 158

Saloon Restaurant 158

Harry's Smoke Shop 171

Twin Smoke Shoppe 171

Anastasi Seafood 174

Appendix A: Featured Places by Category 191

Appendix B: Featured Places by Neighborhood 195

Appendix C: Featured Places by Year of Origin 199

Photo Credits 202

Bibliography 203

Index 204

About the Author

A born and raised Pennsylvania girl, Tanya Birch began her writing career as a teenager, when she won two national and three state Gold Scholastic Awards for writing dramatic scripts. Throughout college and after, her writing continued as a hobby, but she was "sidetracked" by ten years of financial services careers in New York City. That all changed in 2012 when Tanya moved to London, England, and homed in on her passion, creating a successful blog, *Pennsylvania Girl Abroad* (pagirlgoesabroad.com), where she traveled to over 20 countries and shared her memorable stories through her writing. Now back in the US, she's more than excited to write about all the inspiring stories out there closer to home.

Acknowledgments

Words can't truly express my gratitude to my husband, Jim, who supported me emotionally, financially, and in countless other unforeseen ways as I pursued this path toward a new profession, especially the writing profession, which (at least for the time being) is way less secure and financially viable than the one I had when he married me.

To my parents (Lori and Rich, Bryon and Mary), grandparents (Carol and Lee), and sister, Lindsey, who have always supported me, told me they were proud of me, and trusted me in anything I've pursued. Special thanks to my mom, Lori, who will always be my No. 1 supporter and who has devoted her time, energy, and love to me and to our entire family. She's also usually the one who does all the worrying for our entire family, so we don't have to.

Thanks to my dear friend Tony (my honorary brother), and his partner, Alex, for giving me a key to their Philadelphia house and for letting me become a temporary roommate—the worst kind of roommate ever, the one who shows up unexpectedly and doesn't pay rent.

To my father-in-law, David, who graciously helped me understand the legal language behind my first official book contract.

To my editor at Globe Pequot, Tracee Williams, for taking the risk to work with a new writer. I appreciate your reading that first e-mail I sent pitching myself. I hoped there'd be a tiny chance that someone might actually read it. I couldn't have asked for a better person to do that than you.

To all my wonderful friends who have encouraged me to keep writing, who have devoted hours of their lives to reading and critiquing that writing, often when it was particularly bad and mediocre, especially Michael Hew, Sandy Jimenez, and Mirkka Jokelainen.

To the people who offered their valuable insights and contributed to my research for this book and who, based on their expert knowledge of all things Philadelphia, helped me to find some of those "hidden" spots that I otherwise may have overlooked, including Marcy Hetelson, Cara and Jenea on the Visit Philly team, David Auspitz, Michele Gambino, and some great contacts I spoke to at the Independence National Historic Park and at the Historical Society.

Lastly, I want to thank all the business owners who have taken time out of their busy days to spend an hour or two with me along the way, to share their stories that are admirable and, above all, inspirational.

I'm so lucky to have the opportunity to write about it.

Introduction

J never appreciated the area where I was born and raised, a small town in the state of Pennsylvania. With a population of 1,500, a view of nothing but cornfields from my house, and a location smack in the middle of a few mountain ranges, the town was seemingly far away from the action and liveliness of big cities like Philadelphia (but in reality it was only a two-hour drive southeast).

My original associations with Philadelphia bordered on the less lively side, confined by annual school field trips to the city's museums and historical sites, where I reluctantly followed the group tour through Independence Hall, saw where the Declaration of Independence and Constitution were signed, then posed for a picture in front of the Liberty Bell. All of this "action" was then followed up with a journey through the Betsy Ross House, where we spent what seemed like hours watching a Betsy Ross impersonator sew a flag.

Inside Betsy Ross's house, I longed to get outside, to walk the streets of the city, relish the vibrant city lifestyle, and feast on a cheesesteak. Luckily, this project gave me that chance.

This book is not about museums or about visiting tourist attractions like Independence Hall. It's about other kinds of establishments, all tourist attractions in their own right. The kinds that involve doing the things that most everyone in the world loves to do: Eat. Drink. Shop. And maybe even relax a little.

It's about businesses that opened when the population was half the size it is today. The ones that opened before sports teams like the Philadelphia Phillies or Philadelphia Eagles even existed. The ones that sustained depressions, economic downturns, neighborhood changes, and plenty of other obstacles, but kept their businesses going. These establishments have their own place in history.

As a result of writing this book, I've developed a new admiration for Pennsylvania and a newfound sense of pride for Philadelphia, the largest city in my home state. It was not easy to narrow this list down to 50 spots, but I hope the various establishments I chose will give you a great starting point.

The majority of the places are old; approximately 35 out of the 50 featured establishments have been part of Philadelphia's business community for 75 years or longer. Many are family-owned businesses, now run by third-, fourth-, or even fifth-generation family members. All are discernibly Philadelphia.

They are classic restaurants and delis that make your mouth water, the ones that are the reason why the term *food craving* was invented. In these places you can stuff yourself with scrumptious hoagie sandwiches, classic Philly cheesesteaks, and meaty deli creations.

They are old historic bars where famous writers, musicians, film stars, and revolutionary political figures have been sighted, where people have gone to relax, socialize, and enjoy a beer continuously for the last 100-plus years. Bars like these are often hard to leave because you're having so much fun inside . . . just ask the ghosts who are rumored to still linger there.

They are specialty shops, like a local South Philly neighborhood spot focused on men's and boys' clothing, a historic kitchen supply store, and a flag store across from Betsy Ross's house.

The people behind these establishments are all experts at their jobs. They are butchers, bakers, artists, craftsmen, and chefs. Many of the people can share stories of their grandparents and great-grandparents who arrived at Ellis Island in the late 1800s and early 1900s, then traveled to Philadelphia to find work.

Through this journey, I've seen the many personalities of Philadelphia, of Pennsylvania, that I never knew existed. I've listened to stories about the hard-working people who developed foundations and businesses in this city, making it their home, capturing what the American Dream is all about. I encourage you to read along, then explore this part of "vintage" Philadelphia for yourselves and discover everything you've been missing.

BASSETTS ICE CREAM

45 N. 12TH ST., READING TERMINAL MARKET

PHILADELPHIA, PA 19107

(215) 925-4315 • BASSETTSICECREAM.COM

It Keeps Churning and Churning

*I*t's more than just plain old boring vanilla. In fact, the classic vanilla at Bassetts Ice Cream ("Bassetts") is conceivably one of the most exciting vanillas out there in the ice-cream world. With ingredients like Madagascar bourbon vanilla beans and a rich butterfat, you'll be hooked from your first spoonful.

At the Bassetts retail location based in the Reading Terminal Market (the "Market"), you will also have your choice of all kinds of scooped flavors that Bassetts distributes both domestically and internationally. Flavors include more common ones like mint chocolate chip, chocolate, and peanut butter swirl, to more diverse ones like the green tea and pomegranate-blueberry crunch, two popular sellers in China.

Churning out the right flavors with the right sort of quality and consistency is all part of a great business model, but it takes more than that to keep churning for as long as Bassetts.

Prepare yourself for a brain freeze with these next few tidbits. Bassetts began in the year 1861, holds the privileged title of "America's oldest ice cream company," and is the only one of the original establishments remaining at the Market today.

An ice cream cone–shaped sign and the smell of sweetness welcome you inside the Market at the Bassetts stall. If you can, snag a stool at one of the five round counter stools, where you can watch the history of Bassetts on the television in front of you and admire the original marble counter.

If you can't, don't worry. The stall is not swanky, nor does it need to be, because it's part of the Market, one of the most spectacular indoor farmers' markets in the country. It's been operating since 1892, ever since the Philadelphia & Reading Railroad Company agreed to build a market underneath its new rail terminal. Recently named one of the "2014 Great Public Spaces in the United States" by the American Planning Association, the Market is a treasured asset to the city of Philadelphia. As the oldest stall in the market, Bassetts holds an important spot in its history.

While you eat your ice cream, stroll through the grid-patterned market, checking out all the merchants' stands. Sample hand-rolled cookies, Amish soft pretzels, or Italian pastries. Shop for flowers, cookbooks, French linens, jewelry, or art.

Surrounded by all this goodness, as well as other nearby attractions like the Pennsylvania Convention Center, Center City shopping areas, City Hall, and theaters, tourists are easily attracted to this section of Philadelphia.

It wasn't always based in such an amazing location. In the 1980s, before the Pennsylvania Convention Center existed, the neighborhood's porn shops and peep shows outweighed the family-friendly

tourist attractions, meaning it was not exactly the ideal spot to visit when you wanted to treat your family to some ice cream.

Through these and other rougher times, the Bassetts retail location survived.

Lewis Bassett, a Quaker schoolteacher, founded the company in 1861. He made ice cream in his backyard in Salem, New Jersey, using a mule-turned churn. By 1885 he established a retail location on 5th and Market Streets in Philadelphia, and by 1892 moved it to a new, and current, home within the Market.

Ownership has been passed down from generation to generation, and many in the Bassett family have learned a little something about the trials and tribulations of a business entrepreneur. One of those men was Lewis Lafayette Jr., who stepped into entrepreneurship in 1925 at the age of only 21; it was a heavy weight on his shoulders to continue the business that his grandfather began over 60 years earlier. Then there's Ann Bassett, who stepped in during the company's largest expansion in its history in the mid-1970s, when she helped introduce Bassetts products to reputable grocery stores and restaurants across the Northeast and eventually to other states.

I had the pleasure of speaking to Ann's son, Michael Strange, the president since 1989 and great-great-grandson of the founder. I also met with Roger Bassett and his son, Eric. Roger, like Michael, is also a great-great-grandson of the founder, in charge of running the retail location.

Michael and Roger were involved in the business from a young age. They started working as teenagers, when, among other tedious tasks, they wiped counters, restocked ice cream, and cleaned lids.

Both entrepreneurs at heart, Michael worked in the corporate world for a few years after college until he decided to join the family business full time. Roger juggled college life and work simultaneously, a similar path to the one his son Eric is following today, balancing his classes at Drexel University with his work at Bassetts.

Roger's love for entrepreneurship evolved into creating a separate business in 1983, a business centered on selling hand-carved turkey and turkey sandwiches. It exists today as the Original Turkey.

But it was not all smooth sailing. There were a few mistakes along the way, like the time they tried to launch a self-serve sundae bar at

the Bassetts Market location. That was quite the "messy" mistake, literally.

As a result of those lessons learned, Roger's mantra today is "Keep it simple." Michael, on the other hand, has a slightly different plan for the future of the retail business, one that's usually a little "less simple," as can be proven from his recent wholesale expansion into the Chinese marketplace and new product creations like ice-cream cake and ice-cream sandwiches.

As we wrapped up the interview, Roger restated his strong opinion on continuing to sell "scoops only" at the retail stall. Michael chimed in, "I still think ice-cream cakes could work."

Whoever wins this battle doesn't really matter. It will all work out. You really can't expect anything less from a strong, entrepreneurial family who's figured out how to keep the family business going for over 150 years.

BOB & BARBARA'S LOUNGE

1509 SOUTH ST. • PHILADELPHIA, PA 19146

(215) 545-4511 • BOBANDBARBARAS.COM

Jazz, Drag & Even Karaoke

*J*t was once a street to visit for your garment and fabric needs. It became a street to go to for all-night partying, to get a tattoo, buy a bong, or have your palm read. It was frequented by hippies, then later hipsters. South Street today has turned into a Philadelphia tourist destination, where you can still party and go barhopping, but where you can also get a Starbucks coffee and purchase your fresh organic produce from Whole Foods. In the midst of all this change, there is a "beacon of old" that stands out, beckoning you in from the corner of 15th and South Streets.

Well, let's get this straight. It doesn't really beckon you in. From the outside there's an unattractive caged-in window, one lone sign that reads Bob & Barbara's Lounge, and a ramp up to the main entrance. It's suspicious looking yet still enticing, luring you to take a closer look.

Take a closer look at the pictures on the sign and you get a sneak preview of what's to come. One of those is a painting of music notes.

On Friday and Saturday nights, music notes may come in the form of jazz and blues music reverberating from the party inside. A Hammond B-3 organ is the key attraction. The organ itself, made up of two 61-note keyboards, was most popular in the '50s and '60s. Next to the organ, there's a tenor saxophone and a set of drums. The musicians playing these instruments on a Friday night, the Crowd Pleasers, have likely been playing their "liquor drinking" music since the '50s and '60s. Live jazz shows that have been running as long as

this one in the city of Philadelphia are few and far between, especially ones with no cover charge to get inside.

Step into Bob & Barbara's Lounge on a Thursday night, and you'll get a different type of show, another long-running performance entertaining the crowds for over 20 years. Miss Lisa hosts Philadelphia's longest-running drag show, and all are welcome: straight, gay, or otherwise.

On other nights of the week, you have the opportunity to observe an open-mike night or occasionally even a live country-music band. You have the chance to show off your own performance skills at karaoke.

For many participants, karaoke often involves some liquid courage before taking the stage. To get that, you may want to consider the bar's bestseller, Pabst Blue Ribbon ("PBR"). It's easy to recognize that PBR is a popular drink from the exterior of the bar alone; on both sides of the bar's sign, there are two other signs advertising PBR. Inside the bar, you will be surrounded by what might be one of the world's largest collections of vintage Pabst Blue Ribbon memorabilia outside of the PBR headquarters. The bar's current owner, Jack Prince, is a scout for all things Pabst, and he often can be found at an auction or antique sale ready to purchase the next great piece

Vintage Spot: Bar

MCGLINCHEY'S BAR: EST. 1968

In the midst of upmarket Rittenhouse Square hotels, trendy wine bars, and eclectic craft-beer bars, there is one place you can go to get a full pitcher of beer for less than the cost of one pint at most other places in the neighborhood. It also has a jukebox, a laid-back attitude, and a smoke-filled atmosphere. Cigarette smokers especially welcome.

259 S. 15th St.; (215) 735-1259; mcglincheys.com

of memorabilia. All of this Pabst stuff is fitting. Leonard "Butchie" Dwight, the day bartender for the last 10 years, told me that they "sell more PBR beer than the whole Eastern Seaboard." An order for 100 thirty-packs of beer per week is not uncommon.

All of this Pabst Blue Ribbon stuff also plays an important role in the drink that has made Bob & Barbara's Lounge famous. That drink is called the Special, where for a cost of $3, you can get a can of Pabst and a shot of Jim Beam. A previous manager named Rick D. invented The Special about 20 years ago, while the bar was still under the ownership of its namesakes, Robert Porter and Barbara Carter. It became so famous throughout Philadelphia that other bars all started creating their own versions of the special, naming their versions the Citywide Special.

When I stopped by in the midafternoon on a quiet weekday, there were two customers drinking The Special. Otherwise it was low-key, dark, and calm. You are immediately transformed back into the year 1969, where a burgundy-colored puffy padding trims the bar. Padded barstools match the bar trimming, worn from so many years of use. Tacky green, red, and yellow circular hippie-style lights hang from the ceiling. Silver cash registers are still used. (By the way, this bar is cash only, so come prepared.) The only newish thing inside the place is a flat-screen television and a jukebox. Otherwise, like this book's title alludes, it's clearly vintage.

The crowd could sometimes also be described as vintage, too, if you're associating the term *vintage* with the term *old*. One afternoon, Butchie might serve an 81-year-old man enjoying his afternoon Yuengling Lager at the bar, while just a short time later, he'll serve a group of college kids out to celebrate a 21st birthday. That's what makes it fun. He loves this place and explains, "Every day I wake up, I look forward to coming in here because I don't know what the hell I'm going to see."

BOMB BOMB BBQ GRILL & ITALIAN RESTAURANT

1026 WOLF ST. • PHILADELPHIA, PA 19148

(215) 463-1311 • BOMBBOMBPHILLY.COM

Explosion of Flavors

*I*t's not an error—grammatical or spelling or otherwise. It was meant to contain the word *bomb* in its name, written twice. It was also meant to integrate two very different food categories into its name. Confused yet? That's what makes the story of Bomb Bomb BBQ Grill & Italian Restaurant an extra-special one.

Hearing the word *bomb* usually makes you think of a very negative situation, most often as a result of war or terrorism. That's why it was a crazy occurrence when a bomb went off in an unlikely spot, in what was a quiet South Philly neighborhood in 1936. This bomb was the result of a war, not between countries or religious organizations, but by business rivals who were jealous of the taproom at Warnock and Wolf Street owned by Vincent Margarite. These rivals placed a bomb on the steps of the taproom in February 1936 to encourage Vincent to leave. He didn't. A day later he reopened the taproom, and about two months later, there was another surprise attack, another bomb, this time stronger, causing many neighbors to be thrown from their beds, including Vincent and his family who lived in an apartment above the taproom. Eventually Vincent was forced to give into the pressure from both his rivals and his neighbors, who were worried there'd be another, even bigger, bomb, and the taproom closed. It then reopened as a tavern owned by Jimmy Cataldi, which was a successful business for many years.

In 1951, Frank Sabato Sr. purchased the tavern. The locals were still calling the place "Bomb Bomb" because of what happened 15

years earlier, so Frank gave into the name and called it Bomb Bomb Tavern. He is probably one of the only people who have figured out how to turn the word *bomb* from a negative into a positive, because now, almost 65 years later, it is still a successful operation owned by the Sabato family, having outlasted many other businesses in the neighborhood that have come and gone.

Frank Jr. (Frank's son) took over in 1990 and is now running the place along with his wife, Deb. Upon entering, you'll see a bar with about six or seven barstools and a few cocktail tables. It's homey and comfortable, where the bartenders often call customers "honey" and treat you like one of the family. If you visit on a few occasions, you will likely see the same bartenders, servers, and chefs; most have been working there for an average period of 15 years.

A wooden wall divides the bar section from the restaurant, a small casual, intimate space with green-painted walls, deep-brown tables, and seating for approximately 30 people. It's the type of space that doesn't offer much intimacy in the form of a private conversation, but it does allow you to become more intimate with other customers sitting nearby. Some of the regular customers who visit today have the evidence to prove this intimacy: Many longtime friendships have developed at this restaurant.

It was Frank Jr. and Deb's decision to expand on the restaurant's name and weave two very diverse food categories—barbecue and Italian—into one successful restaurant operation. Their reasoning was simple. There were many Italian restaurants in the neighborhood when Frank and Deb took over, so they knew they needed to create something unique to set it apart. After enjoying baby back ribs at the then-famous restaurant chain Rib-Its (the original of which was in Old City on South 2nd Street in the '80s), they knew they could bring that type of food to this small South Philly neighborhood. They experimented with their own homemade sauces and rubs until they found the perfect combination, then renamed the place Bomb Bomb BBQ Grill.

But there was a slight problem: They were amazing Italian cooks living in a neighborhood with lots of other Italians who still wanted Italian specialties.

Frank Jr. and Deb both grew up in the same South Philly neighborhood and knew how to create wonderful homemade Italian food from the recipes that they learned from previous generations. So they came up with another simple solution that's served them well to this day: Incorporate the words *Italian Restaurant* at the end of the name. It worked.

Today at the restaurant you can choose from a menu of crab cakes, mussels, or a full rack of barbecue ribs. When I showed up at around 10 in the morning, Deb was hard at work in the kitchen with other chefs, creating all the homemade goodness that goes into their meals, while Frank Jr. was out at the seafood markets, where he shops for fresh seafood at least five days of the week.

Frank Jr. has lived and breathed the restaurant and bar business. He even lived above the restaurant the first two years of his life. After high school, at the age of 19, he joined the business full time because his dad needed help. He's been there ever since. At one time in his life, while it was still Bomb Bomb Tavern, the place was popular with the beer-and-shot men who would frequent the place as soon as it opened at 8 a.m. On days that Frank Jr. was a little late to work, he'd get a personal wake-up call from the regular customers who knew where he lived. They'd knock on the door of his home to wake him up and ask him to open the restaurant.

Today Frank Jr. has figured out a way to separate work and personal time. Gone are the days when patrons knock on his door. Maybe that's because he moved out of this South Philly neighborhood to New Jersey many years ago, where the regulars can't easily knock on his door anymore.

Regardless what the reason is, it's still the place where there are many regular customers, familiar faces, and hearty food. Frank Jr. describes it as the feeling of "eating in your grandmother's kitchen." If you're one of the old-time customers in this Italian American neighborhood, there's only one small detectable flaw with this statement: Most Italian grandmothers I know don't regularly make delicious racks of barbecue ribs.

CACIA'S BAKERY

1526 W. RITNER ST. • PHILADELPHIA, PA 19145

(215) 334-1340 • CACIABAKERY.COM

Rolling in the Dough

𝓷 ot the money kind, but the real kind of dough, as Cacia's Bakery is especially known for their amazing blackboard of doughy creations like bread, dinner rolls, pizza, and stromboli. Also for their annual turkey tradition. That story will come later.

Cacia's makes everything from scratch. At the beginning of any basic bread-making process, there's some mixing involved to get to the right combination of key ingredients like flour, water, yeast, and salt. The real mixing at Cacia's began around the year 1953, when Sam Cacia purchased a bakery on West Ritner Street in South Philly. The original owner had two sons, who did not want to be bakers, so he sold it to Sam, who fortunately had sons who wanted to be bakers. Sam Cacia knew he had a great foundation in the brick oven built in 1944. That same brick oven is still used today. Sam passed away at an early age, in his late 40s, and there was a great deal of speculation then as to what would happen with the bakery, and if one or all of the three sons would be able to take on the enormous responsibility of the bakery business without their father's guidance. They did. Today two out of the three sons are still bakers. One of the sons has branched off to operate Cacia's locations in New Jersey and Delaware County, Pennsylvania. The other son, Joe, and Joe's son, also named Sam, are in charge of the original South Philly location.

The current owner, Sam, began working at 12 years old. From a young age, he learned the process so he could perfect the art and knead it in the most efficient way. After school on Friday, he started

13

his baking career by contributing to other tasks necessary to run the business, like taking phone orders and boxing pizzas.

Just as bread takes time to rise, it takes time for a boy to develop into a leader. Sam was the quarterback of his high school football team, and that was the start of developing his leadership skills. A quarterback has to lead a team in the same way a business owner has to lead a company. Sam never really gave serious thought to pursuing any other profession. When I asked if he still likes what he's doing, his response is brief and to the point: "If I didn't like it, I wouldn't be here every day. I like being able to call the shots."

The family business operated out of its sole location in South Philly until the late 1980s, and today they've stretched out their business to other locations, first in Delaware County, Pennsylvania, then on to Cherry Hill and other New Jersey spots. Their original location has grown as they've purchased additional buildings and joined them together over the years, but the customer space you see inside today is still about the same as it was 60 years ago. The retail space is small but large enough to step inside and look through the glass cases at the pizzas and admire the production space. You can see all the way back to the brick oven at the rear wall of the store.

The brick oven is warmed up for about 30 minutes in the morning and then later heated up again for another 75 minutes to prepare to bake the pizzas. Baking is especially crucial for Cacia's at Thanksgiving time, when they have taken on the responsibility of making sure that turkeys are cooked perfectly for over 100 family Thanksgiving dinners. Customers stuff their own turkeys and bring them to Cacia's Bakery already in the roasting pans. Each is marked with a metal tag for identification, and then it's up to Sam, his father, Joe, and the rest of the Cacia's team to cook all those turkeys in the brick oven. Last Thanksgiving they made over 125 turkeys!

Then there's the pizzas, which take around 15 to 20 minutes to bake once the oven's properly heated. Pizza specialties include their tomato pies. The pizza "gravy" for the tomato pie, based on Sam's grandmother's original recipe, is made every morning. There are also options like broccoli pie, white pie, and a Pizzazz Pizza that's topped with spicy meats and jalapeños. The pizzas have won some awards over past years, including a Readers Choice Award from the *South Philly Review*.

If you're a pizza addict, consider the Pizza Olympics event, sponsored by the *South Philly Review*, where for around $15 you'll get to sample pizzas from various Philadelphia pizza shops and bakeries over a three-hour period, then pick your favorite from categories including sauce, creative toppings, and Sicilian. Cacia's Bakery is a repeat gold-medal winner at the Pizza Olympics.

All this talk of pizza and bread should be making you hungry by now. I encourage you to see it and taste it for yourself. I was lucky enough to visit Cacia's Bakery on a day when they were pulling some freshly baked, delicious-smelling rolls from their oven. There's no greater way to start the day than a warm roll for breakfast.

CAMPO'S DELI

214 MARKET ST. • PHILADELPHIA, PA 19106

(215) 923-1000 • CAMPOSDELI.COM

A Cheesesteak Phanatic

*I*t started in the southwest. It expanded east to Old City. It progressed farther north to Temple University's campus. It took over the Wells Fargo Center and Citizens Bank Park, where it fills the Phillies' baseball park and Flyers' ice hockey stadium with the wonderful aromas of Philly cheesesteak. Plot its locations on a map and you'll understand why Campo's Deli is a noted spot within Philadelphia's competitive sandwich marketplace.

Since 2000, Campo's Deli has moved their primary location into Old City, also known as "America's most historic square mile." You might expect you'd be able to find lots of cool vintage spots to eat, drink, or shop in a neighborhood called Old City. Wrong. There's plenty of great vintage buildings and rich history in this section of Philly, but not many "vintage" eating establishments.

Fortunately Campo's move to Old City gave the neighborhood one. Inside the deli, the timeworn exposed brick on both of the walls is warming, reminding you that you're in an *old* Old City building. The seating is only slightly more comfortable than the seat you might get while you're enjoying a Campo's sandwich at a Phillies or Flyers game, but it's ideal for the old-school sports-theme feel. Small round tables and custom-designed seats boast the Campo's logo, alternating between red- and blue-colored seats. The red seats are labeled with the Phillies baseball logo and the word *Heater*, advertising the Heater sandwich, a spicy cheesesteak with hot peppers, jalapeño cheddar, and buffalo hot sauce. The blue seats are denoted with the Flyers logo and the word *ice*, promoting their signature Flyers Ice

Steak, made with Philly cream cheese, tomato, jalapeño cheddar, and oregano.

A sign above the cash register reads "Eagles Blvd." The Phillies mascot, a large, green puffy creature known as the Phillies Phanatic, has been known to make an appearance at Campo's after rallies. Point is, walk into Campo's wearing any non-Philadelphia sports jersey and you'll stand out. This city is proud of its sports teams and very well should be. Campo's interior reminds you about its hometown pride.

Campo's Deli has had a presence in the city of Philadelphia since 1947, so even though their location is newer in nature, their roots are well established. Ask any resident of southwest Philadelphia, and the probability is high that they'll know of the Campo family.

Ambrose and Rose were the proprietors of the first Campo's, a small grocery store and luncheonette on 62nd Street that developed into a famous little spot in their neighborhood. In 1975, the business was passed down to Mike, who is Ambrose and Rose's son, and to Mike's wife, Denise.

With Denise and Mike's direction, the small grocery store became less grocery and more luncheonette. They enhanced the sandwich, hoagie, and cheesesteak menu and focused in on what the younger generation recognizes today as pure Campo's: a place to go for quality, homemade sandwiches from a born and raised Philadelphia family.

If you can't tell by the name alone, the Campo family is from an Italian background, meaning that you should also consider visiting for the hoagies like the Campo's Italian Special, packed with salami, ham capocollo, peppered ham, pepperoni, prosciutto, and provolone.

No french fries here, but you won't care when there's homemade sides like pepper shooters, which are hot peppers stuffed with prosciutto and sharp provolone, and marinated mozzarella. Or maybe you want to add on a pasta salad, homemade potato salad, stuffed olives, coleslaw, or macaroni salad.

The third generation of the family, Mia and Mike, are now stepping in and taking on responsibilities in the business, especially Mia, who is the familiar face you'll get to know if you visit the Old City location more than once.

Mia knew she was destined for this work. While growing up, she remembers how much she loved playing with a toy cash register, and she regularly recalls creating makeshift stores in her living room. She's a little less excited today about playing cash register since it's now a real part of her job, but she still couldn't imagine doing anything else. She describes it as bittersweet: "When you're there, you complain. When you're not there, you miss it."

Southwest Philly residents might miss the original Campo's, as the family sold it about 10 years ago, but some still make the trek to Old City, where they're guaranteed to get what they came in for: the same quality sandwich that has been satisfying their food cravings since they were children.

In addition to the original customers, Campo's is now situated in a convenient spot for tourists longing to get their first Philly cheesesteak, a short walking distance from attractions like the Liberty Bell, Independence Hall, the Betsy Ross House, and the National Constitution Center.

Within Old City, Campo's is one of the oldest existing family deli businesses. They've figured out a way to take their business to the next level, to keep their roots and their famous homemade recipe traditions while becoming a real presence in the city of Philadelphia among tourists and locals alike. So take a much-needed break after exploring the Old City streets and visit this real live Philadelphia family in action.

CAPPUCCIO'S MEATS

1019 S. 9TH ST. • PHILADELPHIA, PA 19147

(215) 922-5792 • CAPPUCCIOSMEATS.COM

+≡≡+

The Ties That Bind . . . Sausage

In the early days of the business, there were just two choices: either hot or mild. The customer's decision was simple. The process that the Cappuccio family went through to get the products, on the other hand, was much more complex.

Cattle would often be walked in from nearby farming towns, then across Chestnut Street, making their way to the slaughterhouse at Front and Queen Streets. "That was before Chestnut Street was paved," Antoinette, co-owner of Cappuccio's along with her husband, Harry, informed me.

This is one of the many stories she and Harry told me as we sat in the back room of Cappuccio's Meats, a room that at one time was also used as a family kitchen.

The building hasn't really changed all that much. The storefront is almost exactly the same. The wood flooring is the original flooring. The rails hanging above your head are the original rails, contraptions that were used to hang the animal carcasses inside the store.

You won't see hanging pigs or calves on display anymore, though you will see more display cases. Walk past the display window outside and you'll be drawn in, first by the sign—a neon cow's head next to a neon sign with the name of the store—then by the racks underneath, packed with the types of products you can choose. The obvious focus is the sausage, and they've branched out from hot and mild.

New flavor choices—almost 30—are stuffed with different and interesting things, including herbs, cheeses, and vegetables. There's sausage meat made of pork, veal, chicken, or lamb.

Try the *chevalata*, a pork sausage stuffed with imported provolone and parsley; the broccoli rabe with provolone, spinach with provolone; or veal sausage with pepper and onion. There's chicken sausage with apple cinnamon, turkey sausage with sage, or a Spanish-style chorizo. For the wine lovers, try the Sicilian sausage with wine. For the beer lovers, try the beer-and-garlic variety.

Though sausage is the store's signature product, you can also purchase custom cuts of many other kinds of meat, including beef, veal, pork, lamb, goat, and fresh or dry-aged steaks.

Cappuccio's Meats is a corner store, packed in among the many other butchers, cheese stores, grocers, and restaurants in this section of South Philly, part of the Italian Market in the Bella Vista neighborhood.

Today the Italian Market is a tourist attraction, one of the stops on the Philly tour-bus route. The neighborhood has diversified. You can also get Mexican food, various types of Asian specialties, even cheesesteaks, as you walk down South 9th Street.

If you're looking specifically for the all-Italian stuff with an all-Italian family, Cappuccio's is a mandatory stop. The Cappuccio's Meats business is still all in the family, always has been. Domenico

Cappuccio came to Philadelphia from Messina in the early 1900s with only a second-grade education. He began working hard in the Italian Market. Domenico married Caterina, and the two focused on their plan to open up a business. There was no time for a honeymoon between opening up the store and getting married; in fact, the span between these big events was so short that their wedding reception was held inside the store.

Antoinette (Domenick and Caterina's daughter) and Harry Crimi were—and still are—the next generation of owners. Antoinette started working at the store at the age of 5; her job was to tie the sausage together. Needless to say, she mastered her sausage-tying skills.

Both in their late 80s today, Antoinette and Harry still come to work every Thursday, Friday, and Saturday. That means Antoinette has been working at the store for over 84 years!

Family members have pursued other professions and have occasionally strayed off the path, but they always come back. Harry, who works at the store every Saturday, is one of them. Domenick is the

Vintage Spots: Butchers

FIORELLA'S SAUSAGE: EST. 1892

An antique brass cash register and old family pictures on the walls are among the relics you'll see as you step inside and wait for your sausage to be weighed and wrapped in a brown bag. Known for their sausage with fennel seeds, this family-owned business has been doing things almost exactly the same over the course of 125 years.

817 Christian St.; (215) 922-0506; fiorellassausage.com

CANNULI'S QUALITY MEATS & POULTRY: EST. 1927

Previously known as the House of Pork, this place is full of pigs. Actual pigs. Throw a barbecue party the right way and roast your own whole pig yourself (available in weights ranging from 40 to 150 pounds) or do it the easy way and pick it up already roasted by the Cannuli's experts in their special ovens. Besides the pork, there's also all the great classic meat selections.

937-39 S. 9th St.; (215) 922-2988; cannulismeats.com

other one. Domenick had a career as a photographer, with a specific focus on wedding photography, for 25 years before he decided to come back into the family business full time.

Above the sausage-filled display cases are framed pictures of the generations of people who have spent their careers—their lives—inside this store, often living above the building. Antoinette moved only a few times in her life. One of those moves was within the same building, when she moved from the third floor to the second-floor apartment after she and Harry were married.

On the Cappuccio's Meats flyer, they describe themselves as "an old-fashioned butcher shop with old-fashioned customer service," but "old-fashioned customer service" doesn't do it justice. They could also say warm service, friendly service, welcoming service, and even entertaining service—entertaining because of the family dynamic that you will see in front of you as you decide among the almost

30 flavors of sausage. It's the kind of service that might even make you miss your own family and all the bickering and lecturing and disagreements that come along with a family.

Inside the store, I watched and admired the scene in front of me, especially Antoinette wrapping up the sausage I had purchased as Domenick calculated the cost. Standing between her son and her daughter-in-law, Antoinette looked small in comparison. Her voice, on the other hand, was anything but small, the large, booming voice of a lecturing mother, still telling her grown kids what to do.

CHERRY STREET TAVERN

129 N. 22ND ST. • PHILADELPHIA, PA 19103

(215) 561-5683 • CHERRYSTTAVERN.COM

Touchdown at the Tavern

*H*ot roast beef was the game changer in the late 1970s. It helped transform the tavern from a shot-and-beer establishment to a food-and-beer establishment.

Like any good American bar, at Cherry Street Tavern today—so named because it's on the corner of 22nd and Cherry Streets—you can eat your roast beef sandwich, drink a beer, and watch football on one of the televisions inside, and though not technically a sports bar, it does have a deep association to the sport of football. Without it, the current owners, Bill and Bob Loughery, may have never fallen into the bar business or had the chance to work with an admired local football coach, John "Tex" Flannery, who bought the bar in the early 1970s.

Cherry Street Tavern began in 1902 when a bar named Dever's was built. A relaxed, comfy-looking saloon, Dever's had white tiled floors patterned with small red and green flowers, a rich-looking mahogany bar, and three large mirrors that extended practically the full length of the front wall. Below the bar, there was another interesting feature that still exists today: a water trough running the length of the floor below the bar. A men's-only bar before World War II, the water trough was seemingly used as a tray when spitting out tobacco. Some even speculate it might have been a place to urinate. Either way, you never had to stray too far away from your barstool.

During Prohibition, Dever's survival skills were put to the test. It was rumored that the bar was converted from a local drinking establishment into a barber's shop. Not much changed physically. Other

than the presumption that barstools were replaced with barber stools, many aspects stayed the same, including the old original mirrors, the tiled floors, and the mahogany bar. Not much changed culturally either. Some regular customers told Flannery that the amount of customer drinking even stayed the same, though in order to get your drink you had to first get a haircut.

By the early 1970s, it was the perfect establishment to become the home of Cherry Street Tavern. The preserved interior features were all there. Surprisingly even the water trough was still there, though fortunately for all of us, the spigots were removed, and it was no longer functionally used as a customer's spitting trough.

Some things had to change.

Flannery had the insight to know that the bar business was changing. New kinds of liability insurance were created, and there was a more serious crackdown on drinking and driving regulations. Bill conveyed that "Flannery knew the days of making all your money on shots and beers are long gone," which is why, in the late 1970s, Bill, Bob, and Flannery added a signature menu item.

The hot roast beef and hot roast pork sandwiches became the mouthwatering juicy and tender sandwiches that still keep customers coming back four decades later. Today's menu additionally includes

cold sandwiches, hoagies, and soups. "Try the chili, it's the best," regular customer Motorcycle Bill affirmed.

Drink selections are your typical, normal bar specialties, while draft beer choices range from delicious craft beer from breweries like Flying Fish or Tröegs, to beer from America's oldest brewery, Yuengling. I was surprised to see Lord Chesterfield Ale on draft, a beer that I rarely have seen outside of Pottsville, Pennsylvania.

This beer selection reflects the changing customer over time. Previously that customer might have been an old man from the senior-citizen home nearby or a factory worker from the garment and textile manufacturers in the vicinity; today that customer might be a young professional or a tourist who just came from a visit to the Philadelphia Museum of Art. Bill recalls times in the '80s and early '90s when the best business happened at lunchtime. Some people would have a few shots and drinks along with their lunch. Some people would come in for their lunch break and never go back to work. Bill often wondered about some of the construction workers that would frequent the tavern, "What the heck were they building when they went back?"

With all these changes, there was one consistent figure: Mr. Flannery, who was a big reason why customers kept coming back. In Bill

Loughery's words, he was a "for the people" type of man. An admired football coach for 29 years at LaSalle College High School (a Roman Catholic college preparatory school in the Philadelphia metropolitan area). A Democrat who was wealthy. A devoted churchgoer.

Flannery functioned as the head coach behind Cherry Street Tavern while Bill and Bob Loughery were his MVPs (most valuable players), full-time employees at Cherry Street Tavern in the 1970s. By the early '90s, they became part owners of the business and worked out a 10-year plan, giving Flannery monthly payouts. When Flannery passed away in November 2007, Bill and Bob Loughery carried on the routine as usual.

During opening hours, you can almost always expect to see either Bill or Bob Loughery inside.

In his early 60s, Bill Loughery is still working nonstop. He arrives at 6 a.m. most mornings to get things started, with no sign of calling it quits anytime soon. I asked if his own children were interested or involved in the business. Bill's response was short and to the point: "They're too smart for that."

CITY TAVERN RESTAURANT

138 S. 2ND ST. • PHILADELPHIA, PA 19106

(215) 413-1443 • CITYTAVERN.COM

Freedom and Food

*H*istory lessons can be boring. Except when you pair them with delicious food and drink while you relax in one of the elegant period dining rooms inside a stunning three-story townhouse building, a nearly exact replica of the one where the Founding Fathers often convened to create the Declaration of Independence. This kind of history lesson is anything but boring.

You get the full colonial experience when you dine at City Tavern Restaurant. Drink your water out of pewter mugs. Look around at the servers, hosts, and bartenders, who are all dressed in period garb: button-down smock shirts, vests, and bonnets. Admire the symmetrical layout in one of the 10 intimate dining rooms with Georgian-inspired architecture.

There are a few odd, almost asymmetrical things about this establishment, like the fact that the National Park Service, an agency of the federal government, is the legal owner of City Tavern. Or that the current operator of the Tavern, chef Walter Staib, is German. When you inspect the details a little closer, you might understand that these oddities aren't really so odd after all.

Built in 1773 by 53 prominent citizens of the city, the original City Tavern was designed to be a "large and commodious tavern . . . worthy of Philadelphia's standing as the largest, most prosperous city in the colonies" (Staib 2009). It was a meeting place for delegates after sessions of the First Continental Congress. It was a center for the sea captains and businessmen who closed their deals over drinks and meals on-site. It was a place for banquets and parties, including

one held for George Washington as he passed through Philadelphia on the way to his inauguration. Unfortunately the original City Tavern was damaged when a major fire destroyed much of the place in 1834, and it was demolished completely in 1854.

It wasn't until 1948 that the planning process began to give City Tavern a second life. Congress approved plans for an area of land designated as Independence National Historic Park to preserve certain buildings and re-create others as sites of national importance. The City Tavern was part of those plans. Fortunately it was built just in time for the Bicentennial, a celebration held in 1976 to commemorate the 200-year anniversary of the signing of the Declaration of Independence.

Chef Staib was not the operator when it reopened in 1976, but since 1994 he's been doing his part to preserve its important place in Philadelphia's history. He is passionate about preserving the traditions of 18th-century cuisine and decided to take on the large, overwhelming task of City Tavern after discovering its enormous role in our society. Chef Staib is a famous chef, TV personality, and writer; he is the host of an Emmy Award–winning cooking show called *A Taste of History* on PBS, and a third-generation restaurateur. Most notably, he's perhaps more knowledgeable about American history than the majority of born and raised Americans.

As Chef Staib shared with me, there were "so many firsts here. New spices, new dishes introduced. Dinners and affairs that were held here." Prior to the building of the Merchants Exchange, City Tavern was the unofficial merchants' meeting zone, where businessmen would congregate to share and trade new spices and goods.

The menu and food choices at City Tavern today are signature 18th-century American cuisine, but like America as a country, they are really a blend, adaptation, and culmination of other cultures, including German and British cuisine and African and West Indies spices and culinary flavors. Observe where the influences came from when you study the varied, exciting food menu at City Tavern today.

Choose from signature dishes like the lobster pie or turkey pot-pie, hearty options made with puff pastry. Visit on a cold or rainy day to warm yourself with one of the homemade soups, like corn chowder or the spicy West Indies pepper pot soup. Choose from entrees like wiener schnitzel, rabbit, venison, pork chops and rack of lamb.

You'll want to save room for dessert once you feast your eyes on the dessert tray, which includes specialties like Martha Washington's chocolate mousse cake or Thomas Jefferson's crème brûlée. Chef Staib is proud that City Tavern is truly a farm-to-table restaurant experience, where even the bread is made in the pastry shop downstairs. With all of this delicious food, there should be delicious drink pairings to go with the theme.

Don't worry. There are.

For the beer fans, try the beer sampler: Ales of the Revolution. City Tavern contracts with local microbrewery Yards Brewing Company (yardsbrewing.com) to re-create the recipes of the Founding Fathers. Thomas Jefferson's Tavern Ale or General Washington's Tavern Porter are among the picks.

For children in your group, consider a cold or hot apple cider instead of soda. Choose from unique adult beverage choices like the homemade eggnog drinks or a fruity explosion cocktail called the "shrub" that is made with champagne and fruit vinegars.

City Tavern Restaurant is a themed restaurant, but it's not only a tourist-themed experience. It's for tourists or locals. It's for Americans or non-Americans. It doesn't matter who you are or where you come from.

That's what makes this place such a joy to visit. After all, this notion of freedom and equality is what our Founding Fathers were trying to promote while they congregated at City Tavern back in the 18th century, creating the foundations of American life.

When you step inside City Tavern today, you will step back in time, with the bonus of a few luxuries that George Washington, John Adams, and Thomas Jefferson didn't have, like electricity and running water.

COOKIE'S TAVERN

2654 S. ALDER ST. • PHILADELPHIA, PA 19148

(215) 271-9487

+≡≡+

A Faithful Kind of Tavern

*T*rue to one of their three common core values of honor, courage, and commitment, these customers are *committed* to this bar. Forget about saying "hi" or "hello" to the other customers when you enter. If you say "semper fi," meaning "always faithful," you'll be more respected.

That's because the typical Cookie's Tavern customer is a member or a veteran of the US Marine Corps, and if you're part of this group, you will also typically have heard about this bar, even if you don't live in the Philadelphia vicinity. For the last 35 years or so, it's been home to one of the biggest Marine Corps birthday celebrations in and around Philadelphia. Based on its most recent attendance of a few thousand people, this celebration is probably one of the biggest on the whole East Coast. For one day a year, a large section of Oregon Avenue around Cookie's Tavern is closed down, and the streets are filled with Marines, Marines' families, and a few others that just want to party. There are so many people in attendance that, since the mid-1980s or so, the city government has closed down the street and used the city workforce to reroute all buses and traffic away from the area.

It's fitting that this big celebration is in Philadelphia, because the Marine Corps organization was born in Philadelphia, at a place called the Tun Tavern, regarded as "the traditional birthplace of the US Marine Corps, authorized by a resolution of the Continental Congress, November 10, 1775." There hasn't been a Tun Tavern in Philadelphia since it burned down in 1781, but that's okay. Cookie's Tavern is there in its place.

You won't see a few thousand people at Cookie's Tavern on any other day except for November 10. On the other 364 days of the year, you might see 10 people sitting at the bar at one time, maybe 20, maybe a few more. But not many more, mostly because you can't fit many more inside. There are about 10 barstools, a small space beside the bar for darts, and the two bathrooms. Sometimes there's also enough space for a few dogs, because dogs are welcome here. Dog biscuits are readily available behind the bar.

Wall decorations are in the form of framed pictures, mostly Marine-related stuff. News articles, pictures of honored Marines, and pictures that customers have sent in to Cookie's Tavern over the years. There's a plaque that reads, "In Memory, 1959 to 1975, 58,479 Brothers and Sisters Who Never Returned (from the) Vietnam War."

Fortunately, Jimmy "Daddy Wags" Wagner was one of the lucky ones who did return home from the war. He purchased Cookie's Tavern from his Uncle Bill Cook (nicknamed "Cookie" for obvious reasons) around 1977 after serving two tours in the Vietnam War. He was a recipient of the Purple Heart, a medal that select military members

receive after they are wounded in combat while fighting for our country.

Daddy Wags was the originator of the annual Marine Corps birthday celebration at Cookie's. It began with just him and a few friends. The next year there were a few more, and the next a few more, until it became what it is today. There is no shortage of stories about Daddy Wags; the day I visited, the customers chimed in to share them with me. Most can't be shared in print, but all depict him as a wonderful and honorable guy who knew how to have fun. During the annual parties, he would often climb up the steep steps outside the building to the second floor, where he would give a speech and jump into the crowd, with no advance notice of his jump. Luckily, the crowd would come to his rescue and catch him before he hit the ground. He knew he was always safe taking risks like that in a crowd full of Marines.

Over the years, many of the Congressional Medal of Honor winners would make an appearance at the bar, and Daddy Wags would help connect them to each other. This became known as "Wag's Platoon."

Daddy Wags passed away in 2002 of a brain tumor, but his daughter Marion immediately stepped in to continue the tradition of this bar and its annual celebration. Marion had worked at the bar from the time she was 18 years old and had a close, dear relationship with her dad. She describes herself as the "son my dad always wanted." Marion loves this bar as much as her father did, and it shows.

The customers inside all think of this bar as an extension of their home. Each and every one of them has their own special seat. Everyone knows their place. Well, not always. Marion is cognizant that "the customers make the rules," which is sometimes great and sometimes not so great. Her personal cell phone will be flooded with messages from customers when they notice a maintenance problem inside the bar, and they all have their own ideas of how to fix it. No need to ever worry about hiring a plumber, an electrician, or other contract laborer while there are customers who will step in and lend a hand.

There's a slow cooker for hot dogs, and occasionally there are soups that people bring in during Sunday football games. There's beer, the "coldest beer in the city," Marion says as she points to an ice cooler box behind the bar that the bartender uses as his bench. Beers like Pabst Blue Ribbon, Rolling Rock, and Schmidt's.

Choose from well-known old liquors and less well-known ones. Blackberry brandy is a popular drink. Some say it goes well with cigarettes.

Smoking is allowed in this bar. An investigator recently came in to inspect the bar and told Marion it was necessary to put up "Smoking Allowed" signs. She couldn't find any signs like that, so she bought "No Smoking" signs and cut the word *No* out to abide by the inspector's regulations.

Televisions are stationed at each end of the bar. Marion is adamant about using the TVs for sports and news-related shows. When Marion is sitting at the bar or working at Cookie's, you'll always see these kinds of programs on the television. But as soon as Marion leaves for the day, the televisions all seem to find their way back to the American Movie Classics network. Marion knows this is a likely occurrence; she also understands that the customers make the rules, so she's not really all that surprised. Anyway, it's fitting at a place like Cookie's Tavern. Classic movies for a classic bar.

COSMI'S DELI

1501 S. 8TH ST. • PHILADELPHIA, PA 19147

(215) 468-6093 • COSMIDELI.COM

Hoagie Heaven

*I*t's an antipasto platter for two stuffed inside a long hoagie roll. Layers of prosciutto and sopressata provide the salty, meaty deliciousness, while soft, fresh mozzarella cheese wedges perfectly in between the meat. Roasted peppers, huge chunks of sun-dried tomatoes, fresh basil, green olives, and the dressing of extra-virgin olive oil and balsamic vinegar complete the wow factor. Appropriately, this sandwich is called the Godfather.

When you walk through this neighborhood of South Philly, you often get the feeling that you are in the neighborhood where the Godfather lived—if he had lived in Philadelphia and not New York.

Maybe it's because of the cultural makeup. The Passyunk Square section of South Philly is more culturally mixed than it once was, but in past years it was inhabited predominantly by Italian Americans. People who have been living and working here their whole lives, along with their sisters, brothers, grandfathers, great-grandmothers, and second and third cousins.

Maybe it's the founder's name, Cosmi Quatrrone, which reminds me of a character from *The Godfather*. Cosmi came from Regae Calbria, Italy, by way of Ellis Island in 1928; he first worked in New York at various construction jobs before making his way to Philadelphia to open up Cosmi's Supermarket & Grocery Store on South 8th Street. Cosmi's Supermarket opened in 1932, before there were actual large, supersize chain markets like we know today. It became a great local store in the community for groceries, with four large aisles of all the basic products you desired, along with a full-service deli and butcher

department. It developed a name for itself in the neighborhood as a mom-and-pop supermarket, complete with an all-in-the-family staff of employees.

One of those employees was Leon Seccia, who worked at the store from the time he was 5 years old. Cosmi was his great-uncle. He learned the business from the ground up, literally, considering he was probably only tall enough to stock the bottom shelves as a young boy. By the time the business was ready to be passed on, Leon was more than ready to step in and take the reins. He bought the business for $1 in 1976. Leon was the boss for almost another 30 years, until he passed it down to his son, Mike, in 2008.

Mike admires all the work his father did, and still does, to contribute to and build a strong business. He credits his father with developing it and transforming it into what it is today. His father is still regularly involved in the business.

Cosmi's is now a destination, a slightly off-the-beaten-path destination, but worth the walk down that path for those who do their research to scout out the best sandwiches in Philadelphia. This small deli has made a name for itself.

Over the years its name has been mentioned in *Maxim* magazine and on MTV. It's a two-time *Philadelphia* magazine award winner for best cheesesteak. A featured spot on the Travel Channel show *Food Paradise* is its most recent accreditation.

Over the course of time, it made the full transition from supermarket to deli. In the 1970s and '80s, customers would come into the deli more frequently asking for their "deli meats to be coupled with cheese and hoagie rolls."

Years later, an unfortunate fire in 1999 caused them to rethink the business, but the unfortunate fire turned into a fortunate way to focus on what they realized was their primary business: deli sandwiches. Mike told me that he and his dad realized that "10 percent of the store was making 90 percent of the product." So in 2000, after renovations from the fire, it officially became a deli only.

Except for a few products they still sell today, like toilet paper, paper towels, and some canned goods, it's all about the deli food. The menu is large, made up of cheesesteaks, chicken cheesesteaks, hoagies, burgers, chicken cutlets, homemade roast pork and roast beef, wings, and soups. There's an array of about 20 appetizer selections, plus great french fry combinations. If you don't want a cheesesteak on a roll, you can get a cheesesteak on a potato. Try the cheesesteak fries topped with whiz, steak, and onions.

Inside, you will see one wall filled with refrigerators that are stocked with bottled sodas, soft drinks, and 2-liter sodas. In what probably could be an aisle next to the refrigerators, there are instead two folding tables and some chairs, a place where customers can sit and eat.

Yet it's not really an eat-in joint, mostly because there's not enough space for it. You can walk in or call in your orders to pick up and take out. Or you can take advantage of the online services like Seamless, GrubHub, and Yelp. The majority of the interior space is devoted to the stuff the staff needs to make all this amazing deli food for the customers. That's stuff like the treasured grill, meat-slicing machines, and large storage cases where the meat is stored.

The goal is "making ourselves accessible for many different outfits," Mike shares. That might come in the form of the walk-in customer, such as a tourist in search of the famous Philly hoagie. Or it could come in the form of a big group delivery order, like the college sports teams and television network that Cosmi's has developed catering relationships with along the way. Often they will even extend their hours as necessary to continue some of those great relationships, which Mike describes as the "little things they do."

Seems it's more than that. It's the little things, the big things, and everything else sandwiched in between.

CUNNINGHAM PIANO COMPANY

5427 GERMANTOWN AVE. • PHILADELPHIA, PA 19144

(215) 438-3200 • CUNNINGHAMPIANO.COM

Music to Your Ears

*T*hey come from as far away as Vienna, Austria, and are delivered to places like Wisconsin or Florida. Their ages vary widely. They could be a few years old. They could be 150 years old. Their value is just as wide a spectrum as their ages. The price tag could include three zeros or sometimes even six zeros.

All of the above represent the type of musical treasures that are inside a humble storefront along Germantown Avenue in Northwest Philadelphia. This is Cunningham Piano Company.

In order to fully appreciate its impact, you have to imagine yourself in a different time. A time filled with Big Bands, swing music, and jazz. A time hampered by the Great Depression and Prohibition and World Wars. A time in which many of the most famous pianists and composers lived, like George Gershwin, who composed the opera *Porgy and Bess* in 1935 on a Cunningham piano.

Today you can appreciate its impact on the Philadelphia marketplace by its size alone. The showroom is a massive 30,000-square-foot facility, along with another 21,000-square-foot building around the corner, of which over 12,000 square feet are devoted to the restoration business.

The first floor of the showroom is dedicated to the many unique types of pianos you will find at Cunningham. There are the grand pianos, the baby grands, and the uprights. There are Cunninghams and their newest design, the Matchless Cunningham, but there are also brands like Steinway, Knabe, Bösendorfer, and Estonia. There are digital pianos and digital organs.

There are even church organs, a newer facet of their business, something that Rich Galassini, co-owner of Cunningham since 2008, spearheaded a few years ago, based on his knowledge of and passion for organs. Organs are an interesting business. As I learned from Rich, if you want to purchase a new church organ, "You'd have to bank about $25,000 per rank." Each rank consists of different types of pipes that create different tones and sounds. A typical church organ might need about 20 ranks, meaning a cost of a half million dollars! Cunningham Piano offers a cheaper alternative for their customers. Digital organs now recreate many of the same sounds, so a client might ask Cunningham to purchase the console for their church, and then put a speaker behind a facade of pipes to replicate the sound, look, and feel of a million-dollar organ.

Rich Galassini and co-owner Tim Oliver are always considering what else they can do to contribute to Cunningham Piano's success. Both passionate advocates for Cunningham Piano, they are determined to do their part in continuing the legacy created by others, like Irish-born Patrick Cunningham, who was the original man behind this store. As you walk up to the second floor of the showroom, you'll see his picture on the wall.

His strategy for Cunningham focused solely on one thing: manufacturing pianos. That was in 1891. The design and quality of the pianos soon put Philadelphia on the map when Cunningham's became the region's most respected maker of pianos. Then the Great Depression happened, then World War II, which unfortunately resulted in some tough times for the piano business. That was around the time when Louis Cohen, who had worked in the store as a piano tuner, took over as owner and reinvented their business model. He began focusing on piano restoration, which not only kept the company in business but also gave a new life to the business. Louis's daughters, Rose and Doris, would eventually take over in the mid-1970s after Louis passed away.

As loyal employees of Cunningham prior to owning the business, Rich Galassini and Tim Oliver officially took over in 2008 when Rose and Doris decided it was time to transition the business over, and their love for the music business is evident. Rich started his career as a music teacher before he found his way to Cunningham. Tim's path went from rock musician to managing a music store to contemplating a possible move to Germany to pursue the life of an opera singer. All this happened before he became a valued leader of Cunningham Piano. Today his job brings him to places he never expected to see, like Beijing, China, where he visits and researches parts manufacturers.

The second-floor showroom is as grand as some of the grand pianos you see on the first floor. It functions as a room for concerts, educational programs, and recitals. There might be 20 people at the concert or 200 people. There's enough space.

Even more open space is found in another building around the corner, the restoration facility. This facility is a spectacle in itself. Though I'm no expert on pianos or the technical elements behind a piano, I learned through my tour at Cunningham Piano that, in many ways, there are no experts on restoring pianos. It's a lifelong learning practice. The inside of a piano is as complex as it comes, made up of tiny bolts, screws, and pins that each have their role in making or breaking the way the piano performs. Rich explained, "It's like adjusting a big Swiss watch."

You'll undoubtedly be surprised at what you find inside, both inside the piano and inside the store. Whether you're a pianist, a musician, or just interested in understanding the complex design and beauty of pianos, you're welcome at the Cunningham Piano store, where you can get a personal factory tour from staff who will go out of their way to teach you. They will often even go out of their way in unexpected ways, like give you a ride. On occasion they've chauffeured customers to the Cunningham Piano Company from the Philadelphia airport or the train station.

Knowing this, you might begin to understand that this is a Philadelphia destination worth finding, but one that won't really be all that hard to find, because if you get lost, you know the staff will be there to show you the way.

CZERW'S POLISH KIELBASA

3370 TILTON ST. • PHILADELPHIA, PA 19134

(215) 423-1707 • KIELBASYBOYS.COM

Smokin' Hot

They spiced things up over the last 75 years. There's now a Hotter Than Hell smoked hot sausage, a Cajun kielbasa, and even a Cajun smoked pork butt on the menu.

There's also all the traditional stuff, and if you're not Polish or of Polish descent, you may want to acquaint yourself with the product names in advance. With names like Bigos, Kabanosa, Golabki, Krakowska, and Kizka, and an establishment named Czerw's, you could be in for a big pronunciation challenge when you place your order.

Don't worry if you don't know it. The Czerw's team, and particularly the three third-generation owners—Dennis, Jeff, and John—will fill you in on the important stuff. They may suggest the Bigos, a traditional Polish stew made with cabbage and sauerkraut. In that stew there's also smoked kielbasa, roast pork, smoked ham, bacon, and roast beef. A handwritten sign behind the counter explains what you should have already figured out about the stew: "Not for Vegetarians." Or they may tell you to try the *golabki*, their mom's homemade specialty, a type of stuffed cabbage.

Regardless of what you order, and whether you can pronounce it or even spell it, you'll no doubt love the charm and character at Czerw's Polish Kielbasa store.

As you walk up to the entrance, you may get lucky and walk past a cracked-open door where you can peek into the production room. You might even be able to spot the smokehouses, but even if you can't see them, your nose will perk up at the smells from inside.

Another door is the customer entrance to the shop, where inside it's simple and to the point. Handwritten signs describe all the products for sale. There's a case filled with kielbasa, a refrigerator where all the homemade pierogis are stored, and an old barrel stuffed with pickles.

A shelf attached to the wall opposite the kielbasa showcases old framed pictures of customers waiting in line to get inside Czerw's. Every year around Easter and Christmas there are lines wrapped around the block, where customers wait patiently for their turn to purchase the famous kielbasa.

Fun decorations inside the store come in the form of pigs: stuffed pigs; toy pigs; flying pigs; a pig figurine outfitted in red, white, and blue attire; a pig on a swing; even a holiday pig wearing a halo and a Christmas scarf.

There's a charming old picture of Jan Czerw, the current owners' grandfather, and a few of his employees sitting in front of the store, on the day he purchased it in 1938. The store's interior is practically unchanged since he transformed it from a horse stable to a kielbasa shop. Jan was originally a butcher in Poland, and upon moving to Philadelphia, he began making kielbasa in the basement of his house until he decided he could create a business out of it. He built the brick-oven smokehouses himself, the same ones that are still used in the shop today. Eventually the business was passed down to his son, Ted, and then to Dennis, Jeff, and John. John remembers working in the store from the time he was 5 years old, helping customers carry out packages and stocking the wood pile, sometimes even getting the opportunity to put the wood directly on the fire.

It takes four to five hours to smoke the kielbasa, and it's all done by sight. It's a special skill to know when to throw more wood on the pile, when to adjust it, or when to leave it alone. A batch of kielbasa from start to finish may take about eight hours.

This authentic store and expert kielbasa making have helped them gain media attention over the years. They've appeared on local news shows, won awards for best kielbasa, and more recently they have been featured on Andrew Zimmern's *Bizarre Foods* show on the Travel Channel.

Czerw's staff prides themselves on maintaining loyal relationships with their longtime vendors. They've worked with the same family for many years to purchase their wood (they use only cherry and apple wood). The family cuts the trees and then seasons the wood for up to six months before delivering it to Czerw's to use for the smokehouses.

Trustworthy, loyal relationships with their vendors seem to transfer down to loyal relationships with their customers: On a recent day John received a call from a long-time customer who now lives in Florida. He wanted to stock up on Czerw's kielbasa to take back home with him. He ordered 60 pounds.

An older couple in their 80s comes in every year during the busy Eastertime and waits. John told them once that they could skip the line, but they wouldn't think of it. It's part of their normal routine, a tradition. John smiled as he shared the story. "It makes all the hard work worth it. It's what I live for."

DALESSANDRO'S STEAKS AND HOAGIES

600 WENDOVER ST. • PHILADELPHIA, PA 19128

(215) 482-5407 • DALESSANDROS.COM

Coveted Seat at the Counter

There are no rules. You don't have to worry that the staff will yell at you when you place your order and you forget to say "wit" or "witout." You can order it with mushrooms. You can order it with marinara sauce. You can even get it topped with pepperoni. You can follow it up with a beer. It's a nondiscriminating steak joint, regardless of your color, religion, or level of Philly cheesesteak expertise.

If you are fortunate enough to secure one of the best seats in the house, one of the approximately 10 barstools for counter seating, you'll get the full experience. If you're even luckier, Carol, who's worked there for 35 years and knows the Dalessandro's way, will be your server. When your sandwich comes out, she'll be ready to get you any condiment of your choice, as well as Dalessandro's signature toppings: four different kinds of peppers including mild hots, jalapeños, chiles, and long hots.

The locals know the long hots as "granny peppers" because the grandmother in the Dalessandro family (who also used to live above the store) made them.

If you can't secure a barstool and counter service, then you can join the line of customers waiting to place their order at the counter. It looks intimidating and long, but it goes quickly and efficiently. There are folding chairs lined up against the windows, where you can sit and wait until your order is ready. However, you will want to stand first and get a view of the flat-top grill, where the meat is piled high,

finely chopped up, waiting be transferred over to the empty part of the grill and topped with cheese, mushrooms, or any other combination of your choice.

It's not the only steak place in this Northwest Philadelphia neighborhood. There's one directly across the street and another a block down. But it's maintained its food quality, its traditions, and its signature counter and barstool experience since William Dalessandro, an Italian American, opened it as a steak and hoagies joint on Ridge Avenue in 1960.

When they moved to their current location in 1961, they released a great advertisement that is still displayed inside the restaurant today, next to the counter on the wall. It takes you back in time, with obvious 1960s advertising and a picture of a man and a woman on opposite corners of the poster holding phones, those big bulky old phones that have a cord attached. One says to the other, "Have you heard the good news? Dalessandro's opens today at Henry Avenue & Walnut Avenue." Then on the bottom half of the ad there is a list of their sandwiches, like cheesesteaks, mushroom steaks, pepper steaks, meatball sandwiches, sausage sandwiches, and Italian hoagies. Next to the ad there's a framed picture of William Dalessandro, a dollar bill, and an original menu, the menu as straightforward as it is today.

In today's society, with long elaborate menu descriptions that often make you reach for your reading glasses, Dalessandro's menu is a welcome reprieve. The menu worked well in 1960, and, judging from the line out the door during a midweek lunch hour, it seems to work just as effectively over 50 years later.

The only thing you might need a menu for is the beer selection. When the new owners, Steve and Margie, took over six years ago, they upped the beer selection. In addition to the regulars like Bud and Bud Light, you can also get a large selection of imports and local craft beers, including Victory Brewing, Lancaster Brewing, Tröegs, and Weyerbacher.

Except for the beer, Steve and Margie didn't change much when they became owners after the Dalessandro family sold the place. Steve had been a customer of Dalessandro's since 1983, loved the steaks, claims he "never had a bad one." He knew that change would only damage the great reputation that the Dalessandro family created, so he did the smart thing. He didn't change. He and his wife have worked in the food business their whole lives and knew that

Vintage Spot: Cheesesteaks
JIM'S STEAKS: EST. 1939

A West Philadelphia row home turned cheesesteak spot was how it all began, the owners selling cheesesteaks out a front window of their home. Today there are three other Jim's Steaks in the Philadelphia vicinity, including one in Northeast Philly and one in Springfield. There's also another one on South Street that was established in 1976 and is no longer affiliated with the original West Philly location. This location on N. 62nd Street is the first and is as authentic as it comes. Modest, humble, and serving the signature Philly specialty to West Philadelphia residents, it's a retro spot in the middle of a residential neighborhood and community.

431 N. 62nd St.; (215) 747-6617; jimssteaks.com

Vintage Spot: Pork & Beef

DiNIC'S PORK & BEEF: EST. 1954

Some shops, like Jim's, start in a row home. Others, like DiNic's, start in a South Philly garage, which was how four brothers got started back in 1954. Today they have their own stall inside the historical Reading Terminal Market. Try the roast pork sandwich topped with broccoli rabe and extra-sharp provolone. It was crowned the "Best Sandwich in America" by Adam Richman of the Travel Channel a few years ago.

**Reading Terminal Market, 1136 Arch St.;
(215) 923-6175; tommydinics.com**

they could continue to run the operation with the same high quality and service that customers always expected from Dalessandro's.

Before Steve was selling cheesesteaks and hoagies from this corner shop in Roxborough, he was selling breakfast and lunch sandwiches from a food cart in Center City. For a long time he was stationed at the corner of 17th and Ludlow. He fed the construction crews who built One Liberty Place and Two Liberty Place in the 1980s, buildings that were the tallest skyscrapers in Philadelphia before the Comcast Center came along in 2007. Steve is way too humble when he describes his work.

Yet as humble as Steve is, the business is even more humble, though that's not to say it doesn't have a name for itself. Recently, Jimmy Fallon stopped by for a cheesesteak. They also received one of Zagat's top ratings for food, scoring 26 on a possible table of 0 to 30, placing them in the "extraordinary" level.

Yet in this part of Philly, a neighborhood full of hard-working residents, on a pass-through route on the way in and out of Center City, it's both maintained its humble facade and developed into a standout spot, a rare thing to achieve.

DELUCA'S VILLA DI ROMA

932–936 S. 9TH ST. • PHILADELPHIA, PA 19147

(215) 592-1295

All in the Family

*T*hey were nervous when Mother Superior called the two young DeLuca boys out of their classrooms to her office and relayed the message she received from their mother: "Your dad is injured. You are to go home immediately." They ran as fast as they could out of the school, through the Italian Market, until they ran directly into their dad, healthy as could be, standing next to his fruit and produce stand. "Get changed, I need you behind the stand," Frank remembers his dad saying to his brother Basil. Sometimes, the family business calls.

The family first started off in the fish business, then they moved into the produce business. By 1963, when a restaurant on South 9th Street went up for sale, their father knew what the next business would be—the restaurant business.

Domenick "Kaiser" and Carmela "Millie" DeLuca—their parents— were the ones who started the business. Today, five DeLuca children are in charge of continuing the operation. Known as "the Boss" because he is the oldest son, there's Epiphany "Pip." Then there's Anna, Mariann, Basil, and Frank.

Frank recalls his start in the restaurant business: He mopped the floors and cleaned the toilets beginning at a very young age. When he would whine to his father about why he was made to do this work, his father would answer, "You're going to be special. You're going to learn to do every job in here so you can never get fired." His father was old-fashioned and worked hard every day to run a successful business. All the children knew to obey him. "We did not challenge my father," Frank affirmed.

The restaurant has expanded over the years. As businesses next to the original property on 936 S. 9th St. closed, the DeLuca family would buy it, cut a hole in the wall, and expand. Today there is a bar in the center room and restaurant space on both sides. The felt wall behind the bar is the same. The woodwork is the same. The bar is the same, commonly known as the "Hello Dolly Bar" because it was built around the same time that Louis Armstrong came out with the song. In the restaurant space there's a brick-wall backdrop decorated with Italian scene paintings and traditional tables covered with simple white tablecloths. You can't help but feel the old 1960s charm still radiating from the place. While I was waiting to meet the owners, it seemed fitting to listen to the melodic sounds of Frank Sinatra from the restaurant's sound system. I smiled.

That smile remained on my face when I had the opportunity to listen to another Frank soon after: Frank DeLuca. This Frank doesn't have a love for singing (though I don't know for sure—never asked him), but he does have a love for cooking. His path to becoming a chef happened rather abruptly. While working at the restaurant one

night, the original chef, known as "Cuz," a man who helped set up the restaurant with Frank's dad in the mid-1960s, stormed out of the kitchen, threw off his apron, and quit.

His father had a solution. He picked up Cuz's dirty apron, handed it to his son Frank, and said, "Get in the kitchen and cook." Frank's been cooking ever since. He was 17 years old then. He's a bit older now.

They're known for their "gravy," or, for those of us who aren't Sicilian American or from Sicily, a kind of homemade, slow-cooked tomato sauce. DeLuca's version also includes meat and herbs. You can't talk about the food at DeLuca's Villa di Roma without also mentioning the meatballs. The meatballs have won their share of food contests over the years, including Food Network's *Food Feuds* meatball battle and contests like the Golden Meatball Challenge, a competition between South Philly and South Jersey restaurants.

More important than the meatball battles are the loyal customers who choose to visit the restaurant for their most special events, like birthdays, anniversaries, and even funeral luncheons. One of their favorite devoted customers told Frank about proposing to a girl at the restaurant. Unfortunately that girl turned down his proposal. Years later he came back with another girl and proposed to her at the restaurant. This one luckily said, "Yes!" Second time's a charm.

Over the years the customer base has expanded and the second and third generations are now visiting the restaurant. To them, it brings back memories of times they spent there with their parents and grandparents.

The restaurant is about to expand again. They are currently planning for major renovations to the interior.

Their family has also expanded. The next generation is now involved in the business. Basil's children, Frank's wife, son, and daughter. Mariann's son. Anna's son. The list goes on. With so much family togetherness at the restaurant, you'd expect they'd take a break from it when there are rare times off. They don't.

While the restaurant is officially closed for holidays like Easter, Thanksgiving Day, and Christmas Day, they spend it together. They have their own private party at—you probably guessed it—the restaurant. It's a way of life, their second home.

DI BRUNO BROS.

930 S. 9TH ST. • PHILADELPHIA, PA 19147

(215) 922-2876 • DIBRUNO.COM

Cheese Moguls and Mongers

For some it might start with a lemonade stand or maybe a yard sale. That first taste of entrepreneurial bliss, where you get to make a sale and keep the profits. For Emilio Mignucci, one of the three owners of Di Bruno Bros., it was a box of lemons. At 10 years old, he learned how to cut those lemons in half, put a candy stick inside, and sell them—for a huge sum, about 25 cents apiece. Every year his grandfather tasked him and his cousins with their own job during the annual Italian festival on South 9th Street. They were able to have their own piece of sidewalk outside the store, under their grandfather's close watch, where they'd sell something. One year it was selling hot dogs from a hot dog cart, the next, a more involved project where they made and sold their own hoagies. It grew from there.

Danny and Joe Di Bruno were the original entrepreneurs, two brothers who opened up the first Di Bruno Bros. Grocery Store in 1939. By 1965, the brothers realized that they needed to do something more to keep their business going, to outlast the competition from the big grocery stores. That's when the House of Cheese emerged.

The three cousins and current owners of Di Bruno Bros.—Billy Jr., Bill, and Emilio—grew up in the current Bella Vista neighborhood, part of a large community of other Italian Americans. The community was tight-knit and safe, so safe that from a young age, the parents never had to worry about walking the kids to school nearby. When Emilio left his house, there'd be a group of five or so who met, and by the time they made it to the school there'd be a group of 20.

Their own pack. And all the owners and vendors in the Italian Market were the babysitters. As Emilio described, they'd be "handed from the Giordanos to the Espositos to the Di Brunos."

For lunch, they'd go back to the store, where their grandparents or aunt would make them lunch.

This little store, 700 square feet, was special. It was part of a great culture that Danny and Joe created. They taught and educated their customers about specialty Italian products the same way they taught and educated their children and grandchildren about the world.

Customers who weren't as familiar with all the amazing kinds of cheeses, cured meats, olive oils, and other specialty products out there in the world might have been overwhelmed when they first stepped into the Di Bruno Bros. cheese shop. Danny and Joe made it exciting instead.

Today's Di Bruno Bros. could easily have that same overwhelming feeling, partly because of the number of decisions you have to make. Maybe you want a certain variety or type of cheese. Options include house aged, strong and funky, ash smoked, or Trappist style. Or maybe you'd prefer to pick your cheese by country, like Croatia, France, Switzerland, Italy, Greece, or Norway. Meat selections are similarly confusing to the less-experienced foodie. Pick from products like gourmet bacon, prosciutto, pepperoni, salami, or sausage. Once you've made the meat selection, you'll have more choices. You want prosciutto. Okay, easy enough. Which kind? Jamón serrano, classic Parma prosciutto from northern Italy, or maybe an American prosciutto, like La Quercia Prosciutto Americano?

The current owners and new generation have figured out how to take the basic entrepreneurial skills they learned from their grandfather to a whole new level. One way they've done that is by diversifying the types of products they carry, no longer only Italian ones.

They've expanded the Di Bruno brand into a larger enterprise, which now includes four other locations and a catering facility. These locations are in other beautiful, specifically chosen neighborhoods in and around the city, including Rittenhouse Square, the Comcast Center (the tallest building in Philadelphia), inside the historic Franklin Residences, and in the Philadelphia suburbs at the Ardmore Farmers' Market.

What they haven't changed much is the South 9th Street shop's atmosphere and character, which looks fairly similar to how it did in the mid-1900s, except for necessary changes, such as replacing the refrigeration equipment and updating the shelving.

Loyal customers are always going to have their qualms when changes are made. "You raised the prices 10 cents. Who do you think you are?"

But there are others who will share stories that make you forget about all the little picky stuff and remember what makes it so great to be part of a family business. "I learned how to eat from your grandfather Danny. I didn't know what prosciutto was until he put a piece in my mouth."

How can they maintain this culture as they expand operations? Well they're trying hard. Many of their cheesemongers are studying and completing the Certified Cheese Professional Exam, a three-hour long test that proves their cheese knowledge is up to par. Every year, one cheesemonger is rewarded with a trip abroad to learn about the business and see cheesemaking processes in places like Spain, Holland, France, and Italy.

Emilio travels often to continue his own education and bring everything he learns back to educate his employees. He's always impressed and excited by what he discovers along the way. Most recently that was during a trip to Switzerland, where he watched a small cheesemaker produce gruyère in the Swiss Alps, 4,000 feet above sea level.

Embrace the new but don't forget the old.

After all, great businesses expand, like families. Just ask Emilio. Three hundred people attended the christening of his first son. Almost all of them were family.

THE DINING CAR

8826 FRANKFORD AVE. • PHILADELPHIA, PA 19136

(215) 338-5113 • THEDININGCAR.COM

Craving Some Comfort

*I*t was part of the routine, just like any other uneventful day. Settle in the booth, say hello to a few of the other regular customers and neighbors, and wait for the delicious, hearty meal to arrive. This day, though, would prove to be anything but routine. Inside the diner, her normal waitress never showed up to greet her, but instead a man in uniform greeted her, a private. That private was her son, whom she thought was still fighting in the war thousands of miles away, at his post in South Korea.

This actually happened at The Dining Car in June 2013. One of those memorable days when all the customers eating there were in tears as they witnessed this reunion of mother and son.

Diners often represent a warm kind of comfort complete with good times and great memories. At least they always have to me. As a child growing up in small-town Pennsylvania, the diner was a fun midweek treat where I could eat a juicy hamburger and dive into a large, overflowing plate of fries. Whether you're from Pennsylvania, the Northeast, or really anywhere in the US, the American diner is undoubtedly a fixture in our society.

The Dining Car is a great representation. You can get your food-craving fix at any time of the day. Literally. The only day it closes is on Christmas Day. Otherwise the Dining Car is open 24 hours a day, 7 days a week, 364 days a year.

There's all that consistency that you expect to get when you go to a diner, like the staff. Beginning with the owners. Joe Morozin Sr. opened the original Dining Car, then called the Torresdale

Diner, over 50 years ago. In 1976, the same year as the Bicentennial celebration commemorating the signing of the Declaration of Independence, they created their own celebration by renovating and renaming the restaurant The Dining Car. During that time more of Joe's family was getting involved in the operation, and today his daughters, Nancy and Judy, and son, Joe Jr., are running the operation. The sense of family carries over to the staff, particularly people like chef Larry Thum, who has been part of the Dining Car family for over 40 years. Chef Larry fulfilled roles in the restaurant, including busboy and dishwasher, before finding his true calling in the kitchen as a head chef. Consistent staff? Check. That may give you an understanding as to why The Dining Car has consistent food, too.

When you're in a family business, you often live and breathe the family business from a young age. Joe Sr. had a different tactic: He never allowed his children to work in the diner until they were at least college age, and even then he didn't force them into the business.

His tactic appears to have worked. Nancy, now general manager, co-owner, and a large part of the family operation, almost stayed out of the business entirely when she graduated from Moore College of Art and Design and pursued her original passion as a silversmith.

After working for some years in the jewelry business, she left and entered the family diner business, very reluctantly at first.

Today she's figured out how to transfer those creative design skills to the diner business. Over the years she's had her hand in everything design related, from creating the menus to redecorating the interior. These skills especially came in handy when The Dining Car moved its home from 8828 Frankford Ave. to 8826 Frankford Ave. in 1980. During that time a new dining car was constructed, still vintage looking and built in New Jersey, modeled on some of the traditional old-school diners in the Northeast. Today the diner has more than quadrupled in size from that original space and includes an additional room that was added in 1986, as well as a market, added in 1989, where the freshly baked goods can be purchased. With 10,000 square feet on the first floor and an extra 5,000-square-foot capacity in the basement where there are offices, training rooms, storage

Vintage Spots: Diners

MELROSE DINER; EST. 1935

There's a light at the end of the tunnel, or in this case, after you emerge from the Snyder Avenue SEPTA subway station and turn the corner to find an old-school diner from the 1930s, open 24-7. Sharing booths is a tradition, and many waitresses have worked here for longer than the LOVE statue has been a Philadelphia landmark.

1501 Snyder Ave.; (215) 467-6644

MAYFAIR DINER; EST. 1932

A classic railcar dining experience awaits you at this place that stands out as "one of the longest diners in the tristate area," over 125 feet in length. Its convenient location in Northeast Philly makes it a good stop on the way in and out of Center City, with very convenient opening hours, too: 24 hours a day, 7 days a week.

7373 Frankford Ave.; (215) 624-8886; mayfairdiner.com

rooms, and the baking operation, it's a large facility. More than 100 employees work there to keep it going 24-7.

As a result, the diner has changed in looks, but if you're visiting for the first time, you will still feel that charming sense of old, classic stuff. If you visit in the evening, you'll have no trouble finding it: The bright, neon exterior lights remind you of something you'd see in the original Las Vegas strip. The interior has kept its character with an art deco design, padded diner booths, a long simple bar counter, and the original acoustical ceiling.

The food menu combines that sense of old and classic with a few new twists. Great classics like burgers, French onion soup, and meat loaf. Breakfast is available anytime. There's the Pennsylvania food staple called scrapple. I encourage nonlocals to try it. Just don't ask what's inside first.

Then there's chicken croquettes and crepes, food recipes that helped make the restaurant famous after it appeared on the Food Network show *Diners, Drive-Ins and Dives* during its second season.

The on-premise bakery is another notable component to their business. Customers love the Jewish apple cake and apple walnut pies.

A full liquor license brings another nontraditional edge to their business. There's beer, wine, and cocktail concoctions like Kool-Aid. This Kool-Aid, a mixture of vodka, Midori, Southern Comfort, and fruit punch, is not for children.

On your next road trip, when you're tired and hungry and searching for that much-needed comfort, The Dining Car is there, ready and waiting to fulfill your cravings.

DIRTY FRANK'S BAR

347 S. 13TH ST. • PHILADELPHIA, PA 19107

(215) 732-5010 • DIRTYFRANKSBAR.COM

No More Holes, Just Drinks

Over the last 80 years, there have been many attempts to shut it down. The attempts always fail. As the neighborhood grows, new people move in, people who do not fully grasp that this bar, this "institution" in its own right (as depicted on the bar's website), has always existed and will most likely outlast many more neighborhood changes for years to come.

This place is Dirty Frank's, a knickknack-filled, fun spot where you can go for a drink or a party. It's unglamorous and unpretentious but never uninteresting.

It has a long, colorful history. Everyone, even the current owners, Jody Sweitzer and Brad Pierce, will admit its imperfections over past years. Like the rumor that the bar got its name due to the hygiene problems of a previous owner, Frank Vigderman, who would reportedly wear the same T-shirt for days on end.

Or because at one time, 50-plus years ago, it had to close down for a short period due to multiple violations for serving minors at the bar. In later years the violations came in the form of other kinds of citations as a result of noise. Jody recalls an amusing picture in a news article written in the '80s in which another previous owner, Jay McConnell, who owned the bar from 1978 until 2011, was holding up stacks of citations. Thousands of citations all with the culprit's name spelled out loud and clear: Dirty Frank's Bar. A petition was passed around that eventually received 5,000 signatures from customers and loyal fans of Dirty Frank's to keep the bar open.

Notwithstanding the citations, there's been other drama. Much of this drama happened over 40 years ago or more, like walls punched during barroom fights and tales from couples who say that their child was conceived in the Dirty Frank's bathroom. You name it, there's probably a Dirty Frank's story on it.

Today, there's less drama but more art. Since 1978, one wall of the bar has been devoted to an Off-the-Wall Gallery. On that wall, there are paintings or portraits from a local artist on display. This display changes about every two months.

Your focus is directed toward that artists' wall first because it's plain bright white, the opposite of the rest of the place, which has every bare inch covered with knickknacks. Knickknacks like colorful piñatas. Antique umbrellas, many of which were Mummers' accessories. The Mummers, at its simplest definition, is an organization of costumed entertainers in Philadelphia, another interesting story in itself, but in this story the important thing to note is they have lots of fabulous accessories, and Dirty Frank's gets to display those fabulous accessories.

Paper snowflakes dangle from the ceiling throughout the bar. Dirty Frank's holds annual snowflake-making parties a few weeks

Vintage Spot: Jewelry Store
HALLOWEEN: EST. 1980

A real hidden "gem," this enchanted-looking store is stuffed with actual gems of all kinds, specializing in custom-made jewelry tailored to your needs. There's no sign outside. You have to know to ring the buzzer on the corner of Juniper and Pine, and then walk down the winding staircase to meet the long-time jeweler and owner of the store, Henri David. An interesting guy whether in costume or out of costume, Henri is founder of the best Halloween celebration in the city of Philadelphia, a tradition that started in the 1960s.

1329 Pine St.; (215) 732-7711

prior to Christmas. Think of it as an adult's arts and craft night plus cheap beer. If you make an extra-good snowflake, it could be showcased inside the bar for a long time to come. Some of the current snowflakes have been up there for over three years.

The bar still feels like a bar from another era, and the bar itself is from another era, as well as the cash registers that clearly note "Cash Only." Still, current owners Jody and Brad did have to make some much-needed changes when they bought the bar in 2011. Jody described it perfectly. Today "nobody can fall through the floor," and the "beers are colder." They completely renovated the floors and also repaired the walls. Both had holes. They invested in a new cooler and changed up the beer. Expect around eight beers on tap, four of which are rotated on a regular basis.

When I was there during the lunch hour, there was an old movie playing on the TV, and two regular customers sitting at the bar discussing it with the bartender. Drinks prices are cheaper than most at other bars around the city. You can get an entire pitcher of a few kinds of beer for $8; that's less than the price of one 12-ounce beer at most bars in New York City. They have their own regular Dirty Frank's Special, a 7-ounce pony beer of Rolling Rock or Miller High Life served with a shot of a Kamikaze.

These kinds of bars get under your skin, and Jody admits that. They "become a part of who you are," she expresses. She talks from experience. She first came to the bar as a patron in 1989 when she moved to Philadelphia. As the years passed the bar's manager asked her if she wanted to pick up a few shifts, so she did. That evolved into taking over as manager, then eventually all the way to co-ownership a couple of years ago.

From the streets outside, you have to know about Dirty Frank's before you enter. It's a destination. You probably wouldn't enter the bar if you were a tourist wandering the Center City streets because you wouldn't know it was a bar. There's no sign outside. Until about 10 years ago, it was only a plain gray building on the corner of 13th Street and Pine. Now it's a painted mural of the famous "Franks" throughout history. Have your own contest to see if you can name all of the ones painted on the exterior. Hint: Frank Zappa and Benjamin Franklin might be two of them, and this contest is best conducted while you enjoy a Dirty Frank's Special and sip on your pony beer inside.

Full of Beef

In the early days of the Italian Market, Lee Esposito, co-owner of Esposito's Meats, used to hear stories from his dad that there were 34 other butcher shops in the neighborhood. Today there's only around 4. His family's business is one of those 4, an old-school butcher shop that's been around since 1911. How has it survived?

Some might say it's because they're "full of beef." Not only full of beef, but also full of pork, lamb veal, poultry, and even seafood.

"Where the people who know meat get their meat" is the slogan on their retail services website. The people who know meat know that when they visit Esposito's, they can't just say they want a filet. They have to specify the filet cut, because Esposito's has it all, including head steaks, center cuts, and the filet tails.

Same thing for roasts. A roast could mean a rump roast. It could mean a petite roast. Or maybe a chuck roast, a bolar roast, or a three-corner roast.

Depending on where you live, you often have to give a butcher a couple weeks notice for a specific type or variety of meat that you want. At Esposito's, you can usually walk in, order it and take it home the same day.

Those who do know their meat will also probably be impressed by words such as *natural, organic, free range, grass fed,* and *Angus grass fed* that all describe Esposito's products, in addition to acronyms such as USDA and HACCP, meaning it's a US Department of Agriculture government inspected plant and they follow a trusted

systematic approach to measuring food safety through HACCP (hazard analysis and critical control points) procedures.

Those less versed in their meat knowledge can evaluate Esposito's by using a more straightforward approach. Walk inside the clean, well-organized store and look around. Simply laid-out refrigerated cases clearly display the meat and price (usually per pound), and a staff member will spend time with you providing any information you need, regardless of how simple or complex your questions are about the meat you want to buy.

Through a glass window at the back of the store you get a glimpse into the large warehouse area where the products are prepared, immaculate working spaces with shiny equipment and organized working stations. Surprisingly clean for a place where you regularly get your hands dirty by chopping and slicing red meat. The workers are covered from head to toe in white uniforms, wearing hoodies to cover their heads and gloves to cover their hands.

Proper procedures are important for a place that prepares meat for reputable and prestigious hotels, restaurants, and casinos in and around Philadelphia (most within a 90-mile radius of the store).

With all of this important wholesale business, you'd expect they might disregard the retail business. They don't. The retail business is their foundation. It's how Attilio Esposito got started in the early 1900s, how he managed to provide for his family through recessions, wars, and the Great Depression. It's how he was able to pass the legacy on to his son, Louis, the second generation, and how Louis was then able to pass it on to his sons, Louis and Lee.

Louis and Lee have already managed to get through some very hard times of their own in the family business. The scariest time was after a devastating fire in 2002. They kept all their accounts through the worst of it by doing what they had to do to keep business going.

A friend in the poultry business helped them out by letting them use his plant during the evening shift on a temporary basis, until they were able to move to a vacant plant three miles away. Within six months after the fire they had the retail store open again. One year after they opened the retail store, they moved the wholesale business back to this building. To meet the demands of their wholesale business and fill up their delivery trucks, they have made some changes to the types of products they sell. They added provisions to the orders like cheese and eggs. Within the last four or five years they started selling seafood, including shrimp, lobster tails, canned crabmeat, and fresh salmon sides.

Lee understands how to pack and unload a truck, just as he understands how to cut the meat, stock shelves, manage business relationships, and prepare for the busy holiday seasons. By the time that he and his brother were around 11 or 12 years old, their father and grandfather decided it was time. "Time for what?" I asked. Lee smiled. "Time to lose weekends for the rest of our lives." For him, it's still the same hard work, but it's changed in other ways. It used to be more physical. Now it's more emotional. There are "days you want to pull your hair out and days where you love it. You go on vacation and you miss it."

The business is bigger, the costs are higher, and the potential for failures is larger. There's a major upside to all this: The achievements and successes are greater.

FAMOUS 4TH STREET DELICATESSEN

700 S. 4TH ST. • PHILADELPHIA, PA 19147

(215) 922-3274 • FAMOUS4THSTREETDELICATESSEN.COM

✦

Politics and Pastrami

*I*t was "Famous" from the start. During those early years it was not the only one. There were other branches in the city, all run by family members. Today it's the only original "Famous" that remains, which means that it's not only just *named* Famous now. It's also *become* famous.

One aspect of its fame happened gradually, over the course of 90-plus years of serving high-quality homemade food in the Jewish delicatessen style. The corned beef and pastrami are favorites, both made from scratch in-house. If you order one overstuffed sandwich for yourself, you will probably have enough meat to make another sandwich for yourself the next day, the day after that, and the day after that.

There are so many options of smoked fish that they can legitimately call it a smoked fish department. Nova, lox, kippered salmon or pastrami salmon, herring, and whitefish are among the varieties. As if that wasn't enough, you also choose a side that might include potato salad, macaroni salad, coleslaw, or potato pancakes.

As you eat, admire your surroundings, an authentic interior look that makes you immediately aware you are going to have the full Jewish deli experience. The black-and-white theme is apparent on everything from the floors to the walls, while the white pitched-tin ceiling above you and the smell of steamed corned beef and pastrami all around you complete the experience. A long mirror spells out the

word *Famous*. It's also old and a famous antique, still the original one from the time that Famous 4th Street Deli opened in 1923.

It's enough to make you feel like you're on the set of a movie. At one point, it really was a set. The movies *Philadelphia* and *In Her Shoes* are two of the films that decided to use Famous as one of their locations.

Before the movies came the politics. This is another thing that has helped make Famous famous. Around 30 or 40 years ago, Philadelphia politicians and lawmakers started something that became a tradition, going to Famous on Election Day. Every year since then,

Famous has turned into the spot for the media to hang out and wait for lawmakers, councilmen, and political candidates to arrive. President Obama even stopped by a few days before Election Day in 2010 when he was in Philadelphia for a town rally.

Before all the movies, politics, and fame, there was just Sam Auspitz, the original owner. Sam's son, David, shared with me some stories about his father. One of Sam's first jobs was selling herring. Surrounded by what looked like massive wine barrels full of herring, Sam would stand in between all the barrels and sell them outside on the street, in rain, snow, or sleet as well as sunshine. Two herrings for a nickel. In return he would get $1 a day, a corned beef sandwich, and a cherry soda. This was the start. Needless to say, when he became the owner of the deli on the corner of 4th and Bainbridge Streets, he already had gained a strong work ethic.

The original picture from opening day is still hanging on the walls inside the deli today. During the earlier years, it functioned more as a takeout deli instead of an eat-in restaurant. A takeout deli that was classy, clean, and crisp, with nothing out of place. In the picture you can admire this as the staff pose around the beautiful displays of food, showing off their just-as-classy uniforms, all men in all-white uniforms with white collared shirts and dark ties.

Sam Auspitz continued his hard work at the deli throughout his entire life, until his son, David, took over in the early 1970s. When David took over the business it was booming, both the business and the neighborhood around it. Queen Village was a trendy up-and-coming spot, and Famous 4th Street was part of it. To be "part of the scene, you went to Famous on Sunday mornings," David described to me.

In the mid-1970s, they added a "temporary structure" to the original restaurant, almost like an interior screened-in porch that you might add to your house. The temporary structure added quite a few more tables for customer seating and eventually was outfitted with air-conditioning and heat. That "temporary structure" is still there today. David ran Famous up until 2005. Today he owns another Famous place, the Famous 4th Street Cookie Company in the Reading Terminal Market.

David knew when he sold the business that the man who would continue would carry on the traditions he and his father started. That

Vintage Spot: Jewish Deli

KOCH'S DELI: EST. 1966

The Koch's sign says it all. It's a picture of a sandwich that's twice as big as the cartoon man holding it, which should explain the type of sandwich you'll get at this takeout with all the classic Jewish deli food. In the University City neighborhood, it's the nearest spot for residents of West Philly, and for those University of Pennsylvania students who need a reward after a challenging final exam.

4309 Locus St.; (215) 222-8662; kochsdeli.com

man is Russ Cowan, a fourth-generation deli owner himself, an expert on Jewish delicatessens, and an owner of a number of other restaurants and delis throughout the Northeast. Russ's daughter, Emily, is now involved, a familiar face at the Famous 4th Street Deli, doing "a little bit of everything" in helping to manage the operation.

They've made changes, but the perfect balance of changes, making improvements that still honor the traditions and character of the deli. They renovated the inside but kept the same overall look, and they extended opening hours into the evening. They've opened another location in Center City on 19th Street between Market and Chestnut Streets.

Their product line has improved. In addition to all the traditional Jewish specialties like smoked fish and meats, they have also added a bakeshop. In sticking with the overall theme, these bakery items are just as massive and oversize as the sandwiches. You can get rugalach, chocolate babka, and hamantashen.

If you have never been a part of the Jewish deli experience, don't be intimidated. You may not be able to pronounce the names. You may not know exactly what you're ordering. That doesn't really matter.

After you see and taste the food, it will become crystal clear why you have to experience the tradition of Famous 4th Street Delicatessen.

FANTE'S KITCHEN SHOP

1006 S. 9TH ST. • PHILADELPHIA, PA 19147

(215) 922-5557 • FANTES.COM

A Chef's Paradise

*I*t's like an adult toy store for cooks, chefs, or people who've always wanted to be cooks or chefs. Regardless of your skills in the kitchen, you will surely enjoy weaving through the maze of variety and hidden rooms in Fante's Kitchen Shop.

Hidden because from the exterior, you would have no idea any of these rooms even existed. It's a shop where you're urged to explore, to go back deeper into the confines of the store. In one room you might discover an Il Bigolaro, an old pasta machine that was patented in 1875 and designed to make a thick kind of spaghetti. In another room you might find gadgets you never knew existed, though you know now that you've discovered this gadget you won't be able to leave the store without it. One of those gadgets might be Pizza Saver bags, plastic bags that perfectly seal your leftover slice of pizza. Or maybe a Fante's Cousin Daniele's Expandable Dough Divider, a contraption with five pizza-cutter wheels that slices dough into perfect equal-size strips. You never know what you'll find inside.

Mariella Esposito (née Giovanucci) has been a co-owner of Fante's since 1981, along with her two brothers, Nick and Daniele, and sometimes she still doesn't know what she'll find inside, whether that's behind the walls or underneath the basement floors. Years ago, Mariella remembers hearing a rumor from one of the Fante family members that at one time another family member was hiding money under the stairway. She forgot about this story until years later, when they had to repair one of the basement floors. Underneath that floor were numerous old tin cans. Unfortunately there was no cash inside, but it was obvious those tin cans were the perfect money stashers.

Though not a biological member of the Fante family, Mariella became an honorary one when she moved to Philadelphia from a small Italian town northeast of Venice in 1964. The transition wasn't easy. She grew up in a town of 100 people and moved to a city of 1.5 million people who didn't speak her native language. Luckily, she found her respite at Fante's. The Fante family was looking to hire a fluent Italian speaker, and they found a loyal employee in Mariella. Eventually her younger brothers would become employees at the store.

She started working there at age 17, continued through college, and then kept working part-time after college while she taught Italian full-time. When the Fantes decided to retire in the late 1970s, Mariella stopped to reflect at this beautiful shop that had become her second home in Philadelphia. She looked at all the great history that came along with it. She saw what this place represented for the entire Fante family, a sort of refuge, where cousins, second cousins, nieces, grandchildren, and other family members would always have a job. She wanted that refuge for her family, too. So she and her brothers

decided to take out a loan and take on the responsibility of this specialty kitchen company in the Italian Market neighborhood.
They had to make some changes. The first was to find a focus.
When the shop opened in 1906, it sold premade furniture that was
imported from Germany and Czechoslovakia. The company transitioned into selling cookware in the 1930s. From there they added
another specialty—fancy giftware—and through the '70s, Fante's
became the place to go for gifts for weddings, anniversaries, and special occasions. When Mariella and her family took over, they decided
to get out of the fancy giftware business and focus on cookware,
which was also important because of the store's history: Fante's is
allegedly one of the oldest cookware shops, if not the oldest, still in
existence in the US.

Though Italian products were one of their original specialties,
today they strive to support other small family businesses around the
world, whether from the United Kingdom, Italy, or the US.

Fante's has a classic interior that hasn't changed much—except
for the floors. Ever hear of Con-Tact paper? The Fante family loved
it and used it like the dad in the movie *My Big Fat Greek Wedding*
used Windex. Or like some people use duct tape. The simple solution
to every problem was to seal it with contact paper and paint over it.
That should explain why they changed the floors.

There was only one part of the equation that Mariella didn't take
into consideration when she bought the business from the Fantes.
Her family was much smaller. There weren't 20 other family members
who could work at the store when needed, which meant that Mariella
and her family would have to pick up the slack. Today Mariella still
works at least six and a half days a week, often the full seven days.
Her daughter, Liana, has joined her. Liana grew up in this store, working the coffee bar from the time she was 12 years old. She went off
on her own path for awhile, to college for chemical engineering, then
lived in Paris and worked for L'Oreal for a few years. Ultimately she
decided her heart was here, at the store that is now more than just
Fante's. It's also the Esposito's and the Giovanucci's, and undoubtedly
will be for many years to come.

FLEISHMAN FABRICS & SUPPLIES

749 S. 4TH ST. • PHILADELPHIA, PA 19147

(215) 925-1113

Odds and Ends

Owners of Fleishman Fabrics & Supplies Stanley and Tricia Fleishman were never really in the costume business, but there was one period of time where they sold them. Dance costumes. Ice-skating costumes. Even theater costumes. It filled up an entire truck when they transported it all from New York to Philadelphia. All in all, it was about 10,000 costumes.

It was not planned. It was not even really something they wanted. Still it turned out to be a win for both parties. The costume manufacturer was shutting down, and the costumes were part of the bundled deal, along with other material they purchased. That deal got them a few new customers who came in to purchase the costumes, as well as the opportunity to make donations to some great Philadelphia organizations who could make good use of them.

Over the years there have been many similar instances, some of them as a result of their interest in vintage buyouts. Other times it is part of a strategy to mix things up, go in a slightly different direction, maybe attract a new kind of customer. In the fabric industry, you constantly have to "figure out how to stay relevant," Tricia explained.

The Fleishman family has been part of Philadelphia's fabric industry since 1936. It appears they have succeeded in figuring out their relevancy.

Fabrics are the big part of their business, which is focused particularly on apparel. It's also linings, buttons, zippers, and belting. It's dry-cleaning supplies and tailor's trimmings. It's filters, garment bags, ironing-board covers, and collar stays.

It's boxes. Boxes for evening gowns, wedding gowns, shirts, and other items. Men's and women's suiting.

If you visited Fleishman's from 1936 until early 2014, you might have had to climb flights of stairs to get to some of these products. Today it's a little easier. Just recently they made a major move. They had to vacate the building they were in located on South 5th Street and, like often in their business, find a new direction. Luckily their route led them right around the corner, one block west, to Fabric Row, perhaps a more ideal spot than their original location on South 5th Street, with the potential for more walk-in traffic from people who come seeking out the designated tourist district of Fabric Row.

In distance it was a simple move, less than one-tenth of a mile away. In everything else, it was more complicated. Visualize a move from a 10,000-square-foot building that was filled to the brim with everything from heavy, large fabrics to dozens of cabinets and drawers filled with miniature buttons and pins.

It's a similar-size space that they're in today, just wider instead of higher. Now there's no more stairs, but there's still some searching to do, labyrinths of fabrics and aisles to weave through. Racks and rows and probably still an occasional ladder to climb if you want a fabric on the top shelf.

Ever hear the saying "One man's trash is another man's treasure"? In a way, this was how Harry Fleishman began in the textile business. In New York he met some guys that were working in the industry. He decided to throw a bunch of leftover fabric pieces and ends in the back of his car and sell those when he got back to Philadelphia. He accomplished that. Then he accumulated some more and sold those, and accumulated a few more and sold all those, too. Until one day he decided to open up a small storefront on 703–705 South 5th St. with some partners. Those partners would eventually all go off on their own to start their own businesses. Harry and his wife, Sylvia, would continue running the business they had started from that location.

The next generation was, and still is, Stanley and Tricia Fleishman. Stanley didn't expect to rejoin the family business. He was living in New York and teaching special education for many years before he came back to Philadelphia in the late 1970s to continue the business his father had started.

Adapting to the times has been a regular way of life for them. It used to be more of a wholesale business; now it's focused more on retail. They're always something unique for them to purchase, like the time they met a guy whose grandmother toured with Bob Hope and went into his basement to find amazing vintage tiaras from the Roaring '20s.

Just as unique as the purchases are the unique, always interesting customers. Sometimes that customer is a nun, sometimes it's a Mummer. Often it's an owner of a dry cleaning business or a tourist with a passion for sewing. Fleishman's has to be ready for everything.

They will. They'll keep doing what they've always done. Focusing on their customer, thinking about how to adapt, figuring out what they need to do to meet the needs of the current generation. That's the fabric business.

FREDERICK W. OSTER
FINE VIOLINS & VINTAGE
INSTRUMENTS

507 S. BROAD ST. • PHILADELPHIA, PA 19147

(215) 545-1100 (VIOLINS) • (215) 545-1000 (GUITARS)

VINTAGE-INSTRUMENTS.COM • FREDOSTER.COM

+════+

Strings Are Attached

They get around. Sometimes they travel around the world to folk and bluegrass festivals, national orchestras, and rock-and-roll music tours. Sometimes they sit in one stationary spot, where they're admired as displays in a personal collection or as showpieces in exhibitions at the Metropolitan Museum of Art in New York City.

Before all that travel, before they were part of treasured collections, these instruments all passed through one particular place, an unsuspecting location in the city of Philadelphia.

This location is a 19th-century Victorian building on South Broad Street first built for one of Philadelphia's prominent families, a building on a street that's now known as the Avenue of the Arts, near the theater district, cultural venues, the Philadelphia Orchestra, and the University of the Arts.

From the outside, there's not much indication of what's inside, other than a barely noticeable glimpse of a sign on one of the ground-floor windows. It's supposed to be this way.

Upon your visit, you ring the buzzer and enter a grand entryway. Look up and you can see all the way three stories up to the ceiling, where your attention is drawn to a gorgeous square stained-glass window.

There's not only just amazing architecture. There's amazing vintage instruments. The first and second floors are primarily dedicated to the violin family of instruments. Continue toward the back of the house and you'll enter more beautifully preserved rooms with 14-foot-high ceilings and towering wooden doors. Rich, wooden display cases in each of these rooms store the instruments. Through glass doors in the cases, you might see violins or maybe violas, cellos, or bows.

Go down the steps to the ground floor and you'll discover a room dedicated to the guitar shop, a room of pure excitement for any guitar player. There's a wide array of old and new guitars from C. F. Martin & Co., the oldest guitar maker in the US (since 1833), located in Pennsylvania. There's also a large selection of Gibson guitars. There are Washburn models, Tilton models, and many, many more. When you browse through the Vintage Instrument's website you will find descriptions like this one:

> MARTIN, 000-18, 1927, 12-fret neck, slotted-head, rectangular ebony bridge, nut width: 1-7/8", long glued side crack; recent professional neck reset & fret service by Dave Strunk; completely original & in overall very good condition, later hard case, braced for steel strings; very lightweight & responsive

That one's for sale for $14,500.

Fred Oster and his business partner and wife, Catherine Jacobs, have a well-established, highly reputable business focused on high-end acoustic instruments. The guitar is no exception. That doesn't mean there's not an opportunity to purchase an instrument for a more inexpensive price. There is. Some instruments are on sale for as little as a few hundred dollars. The price range is as wide and varied as the instruments you will see here.

Admire the banjos, mandolins, brasswinds and woodwinds, and ukuleles. Admire the historical antique instruments that all have found their way to this store on South Broad Street, like a Michael Ignatius Stadlmann viola d'amore from Vienna, constructed in 1801.

To discover the instruments you may find here, you can view two websites prior to your visit, one dedicated to fine violins and another

Vintage Spot: Auction House
FReeman's auction House: est. 1805

The oldest auction house in America is based in Philadelphia, and an even greater shock is that it is still family owned. It specializes in buying and selling fine art, antiques, and jewelry; the items that have passed through its doors include a desk said to have belonged to Benjamin Franklin and a set of rare, early colors from the USS *Constitution*.

1808 Chestnut St.; (215) 563-9265; freemansauction.com

dedicated to other vintage instruments. Know that there's also more available, but the website is a start to your discovery. You can visit the store anytime Mon through Fri during the hours of 10 a.m. to 5 p.m. If you're looking for something specific, it's always helpful to call, in which case Fred, Catherine, and staff may have a number of instruments waiting for you, all tuned up, ready to go, and easy for you to evaluate when you arrive.

A selection like this is rare for specialty instruments, and often impossible to get anywhere else in Philadelphia, the state of Pennsylvania, or even many other states nearby. New York City or maybe Chicago might be the next nearest spots.

It's a niche business, which is why some of the major players in the music industry have stopped by Vintage Instruments, and for good reason. Fred Oster is an expert on all things vintage instruments; he got started as a "folkie" in the late 1960s, playing guitar, then the banjo and mandolin. After he graduated from college in the '70s, he became very interested in the auction scene, and he spent time going to musical-instrument auctions in London, where old, reputable auction houses like Christie's and Sotheby's were running the show. Later in his career he became a consultant to these and other auction houses, and more recently he's become a respected appraiser on the PBS series *Antiques Roadshow*.

He made a memorable mark in the city of Philadelphia, where his roots are, when he opened up his first shop in Chestnut Hill in 1974.

By 1978 he moved to a larger location in Center City, and by 2007 he relocated his store to the Broad Street building.

It's fitting that the shop is on the same street as many of the famous music venues and organizations in Philadelphia, like the Philadelphia Orchestra. When Fred attends a performance of the Philadelphia Orchestra, he focuses on the musicians. He listens to the beautiful music that echoes through the performance hall and mesmerizes a regular crowd of around 2,500 spectators. Finally, he counts the number of instruments playing this beautiful music that have crossed his path along the way. It's a proud moment.

GENO'S STEAKS

1219 S. 9TH ST. • PHILADELPHIA, PA 19147

(215) 389-0659 • GENOSTEAKS.COM

Whiz and Wheels

*F*inding your own individuality might seem impossible when you've lived in the shadow of a famous personality, especially when your father has a reputation like Joey Vento.

To some, he was the crazy man who decided to open up his own cheesesteak shop directly across from the "King," or Pat's, the inventor of the Philadelphia cheesesteak. A bold move considering the "King of Steaks" was based in that exact same neighborhood for more than 30 years before, having its share of loyal and regular customers.

To others, Joey was the man who took his $6 savings, combined that with one $2,000 loan from his family, and turned it into a multi-million dollar business. A man who only had a ninth-grade education but still became a successful entrepreneur.

Joey Vento was also that man who always did it *his way*, even when it resulted in a court case and national media criticism for a sign he put outside his window in 2005 that said, "This is America. When Ordering, Speak English."

They won the court case. That sign is still there today in memory of Joey Vento, who passed away in 2011. From that point on, all that responsibility was passed down to his son, Geno.

Geno may have guessed just how passionate his dad was about the cheesesteak business from an early age, especially when he was old enough to realize that his dad named him after his cheesesteak business, not vice versa.

Joey actually created the name of the store four years before his son was born, inspired by a broken door he found in his store that had

the name "Gino" painted on in graffiti. Joey replaced the *i* with an *e*, and the name was born.

So when the reins were passed to Joey's only son, Geno had a few important decisions to make about how to continue the Geno's Steaks brand and business.

Fortunately, behind the scenes Geno had the help of some amazing people who have been involved in the business since its early years. One of those men is Jimmy "Reds"; with a 40-year tenure at Geno's, he knows all the ins and outs of the operation. Or other longtime employees, like Kathy and Karen, who've been working there for 38 years and 37 years, respectively.

Geno describes his dad as running the business like a "dictatorship, not a democracy," but his approach is different. He believes in teamwork and trusting the employees who worked alongside his dad year after year to run the operation. As a result, Geno is able to get out of the cheesesteak shop and find his own way in life, which sometimes leads him away from the day-to-day operation and more in the direction of his interests. One of those interests is his production company, which has produced plays throughout Philadelphia theaters. Most recently he's also participated in the culinary arts program at Philly's Walnut Hill College.

That program has given him a better understanding of how to run the Geno's Steaks business going forward. Though Geno admits his father was strict and that he was often the one blamed when things went wrong from the time he started working in the business at 17, Geno also still has great respect for so many ways in which his dad ran the business.

One is the focus on their signature food and the quality of their product, still using the same recipe today as almost 50 years ago: seared rib eye, chopped white onions, and your choice of Cheez Whiz, American, or provolone cheese.

Another thing Geno learned from his dad is the importance of investing in the physical structure and equipment regularly, particularly important when the operation is cranking out cheesesteaks 24 hours a day. Since opening in 1966, Geno estimates they've had about 17 new floors and 14 new walls. There's even a custom-made ice machine that makes 4,000 pounds of ice at a time.

Outside the store, the bright neon signage lights up the entire street at night. Geno says that it's sometimes referred to as the "Las Vegas of South Philly." Geno's recently added a new neon sign. The brighter, the better.

When I visited on a quiet midweek morning, I was able to sit inside at the very bright orange-and-blue booth filled with pictures of Joey and Geno with various celebrities that have stopped by Geno's over the years. Geno is still proud about the fact that many of these celebrities have opted to wait in lines like every other average person has done to get their cheesesteak. Jack Nicholson apparently waited for 30 minutes once.

When I get an insider's view of the building, everything's immaculately clean. For a cheesesteak place, this is not easy to accomplish. They pride themselves on keeping it this way, and for engineering purposes, many parts of the equipment and operation are built on wheels, allowing for quick and efficient cleaning behind, underneath, and around the equipment.

So other than continuing the legacy that has been passed down to him, what can Geno do to support the future success of a business that will celebrate its 50-year anniversary in 2016? One of his ideas is to take that "on wheels" concept to a whole new level. Look out for portable Geno's Steaks food trucks in the near future, after a concert or a big Philly sporting event, or maybe even somewhere on the streets of Philadelphia near you.

GOLDSTEIN'S MEN'S AND BOYS' CLOTHING

809 S. 6TH ST. • PHILADELPHIA, PA 19147

(215) 468-0564 • GOLDSTEINSCLOTHING.COM

Looking Sharp and Snazzy

It's not often that you'll find a place that specializes in both Bar Mitzvahs and Holy Communions. Goldstein's is one of them, at least when it comes to finding boys' suits to wear at both Bar Mitzvahs and Holy Communions.

When Goldstein's opened in 1902, they filled a missing spot in a niche marketplace. It was a store solely devoted to boys' suits and clothing. In those early years of business, the standard of dress was a little different than it is today. Dressing sharply was more commonplace. You might dress up for the movies, for a day out shopping in a big city. You might dress up for a theater performance, for a party, or for a special family occasion. Dressing up for church, in many different kinds of religious backgrounds, was also much more important then than it is now; it was a time for suits and ties and formal wear.

Though dressing down has become much more standard in the 21st century than dressing up, the traditional suit for a boy's first Holy Communion hasn't changed. It's still typically an all-white fitted suit. The place to get it hasn't changed in over 110 years either. It's still Goldstein's.

In the early 1900s after Goldstein's was established, Julius Goldstein developed a reputation throughout Philly, and particularly South Philly, for customer service and the wide selection of boys' quality clothing that he carried in his store. Located in the middle of the Queen Village neighborhood in South Philly, they were part of the community. A local store catering to the local residents.

In 1935, a new employee joined the business, a local resident himself from the neighborhood. He was a young Italian boy named Vincent Talotta, who managed to get a job at the age of 8 doing stock work. He, and soon after his younger brother, Pasquale, continued working at the store through high school, when their responsibilities transitioned to sales work. Their work at Goldstein's temporarily came to a stop when they both went off to war.

Years later, when Vincent came back home, he went back to Goldstein's. It was around that time that the original owner passed away, and the family decided to sell the entire business to Vincent Talotta. As it turns out, the only place Vincent would ever work the rest of his life, apart from the army, was in this great local neighborhood store. Under Vincent's ownership, he took in a partner, his brother Pasquale, who joined the business in the early 1960s after his time in the army. Vincent also added a new product line: men's suits and clothing. Goldstein's specialized in working with hard-to-fit kids and men, with the idea that if "we can't fit 'em, nobody can," as current owner Vinny Talotta (Vincent's son) relayed to me.

Today the store has a large selection of men's and boys' suits. Italian suits in brands including Mantoni, Mizanni, and Bertolini. Boys' suits with brands from Michael Kors and Joseph Abboud. Accessorize your suit purchase with fashion socks, ties, hats, and cuff links.

Choose from more casual wear like sweaters and corduroy pants. Browse through the various styles of leather jackets.

During your visit you'll often encounter Vinny, who took over the business when his father passed away a couple of years ago. You may also get to know Jack Rehr, the general manager of the store for the last 11 years, who's worked in the retail business for most of his career. They are the two regular characters that will no doubt remember your face, size, and clothing-style preferences.

With a new generation comes a few changes. One is the elimination of the old-school filing system. Vinny's father used to file all hard copies of the sales slips, filed for each customer by zip codes. And direct-mail campaigns used to be Goldstein's primary source of advertising. It was common to send out an average of 15,000 flyers to customers every season. Today there are still a few select customers who appreciate the direct mail, but Facebook and Twitter are used more. Times are changing.

The physical space of the store isn't as large as it once was, due to a decision to downsize in 2006, but the product selection and amount of products you can get hasn't changed. More importantly there is the same amount of personal customer service. We're "not just a robot at the counter," Vinny notes. It's a physical store where

Vintage Spot: Sports Clothing

MITCHELL & NESS NOSTALGIA COMPANY: EST. 1904

It got its start as a sporting-goods store. It turned into a sports-clothing-focused store when the company was employed as the on-field outfitter for the Philadelphia Eagles in 1933. Today, it's a place for all your vintage sports jerseys, headwear, and classic sports memorabilia.

1201 Chestnut St.; (267) 273-7622; mitchellandness.com

you can place a custom order tailored just for you. A store where there's still swatches of fabrics that you can browse through and choose for your custom-made suit. When your suit arrives, they'll iron and press the suit by hand. They don't gouge the customer; they just offer reasonable prices, with a goal to sell fashionable but traditional clothing that will outlast the trends.

Goldstein's reputation speaks for itself. It's helped them survive as times change and, especially, as the local neighborhood retail store seems to be completely disappearing. So take a step back in time, see how it was done 100 years ago, and discover what was so special about it.

HUMPHRYS FLAG COMPANY

238 ARCH ST. • PHILADELPHIA, PA 19106

(215) 922-0510 • HUMPHRYSFLAG.COM

A Sea of Flags

*T*here comes a point for many of us when we realize we're heading down the wrong path. We are quickly making our way up that career ladder, but we know that if we keep climbing, it will eventually ruin the lifestyle we want to lead. For the owner of Humphrys Flag Company ("Humphrys"), Timothy O'Connor, it wasn't a ladder. It was a ship.

He was a merchant mariner for about 10 years when he made the career change.

Timothy's parents helped him make a connection with Harry Spellman, an associate whom his parents regularly did business with through the gift shop they set up while they were the live-in caretakers at Carpenters' Hall (an important site of historical significance that hosted the First Continental Congress in 1774). Harry was the previous owner of Humphrys, a company that already held a long-established history: It was started by two brothers in New York who moved their business to Philadelphia in 1864.

Timothy's parents knew Harry wanted to sell the 100-year-old business and, likewise, knew that their son wanted a career that would allow him to spend more time with his family, so it made sense.

From merchant mariner to flag company owner, which also—strange as it may sound—made sense. From the experience Timothy acquired traveling the world and stopping at countless ports, he learned firsthand about other country's flags. From the problem-solving capabilities he developed on the ship, he was able to tackle

95

the scientific and mathematical formulas required to construct or repair tough flag-manufacturing projects.

Timothy established a manufacturing base in Pottstown, Pennsylvania, then equidistant between his wife's teaching job near Reading and the flag shop in the city of Philadelphia.

Under his leadership, in the late 1970s, Timothy decided to move the retail shop to a new location, one that undoubtedly made perfect sense. He bought a building at the address of 238 Arch St., directly across the street from the house where, reportedly, the American flag was created. Betsy Ross's house.

Today, the flag showroom is in the ideal location to attract curious tourists who, after a visit to the Betsy Ross House, are drawn in by all the flags on the building's exterior. Inside that showroom, there's a good chance you might be greeted by Matt O'Connor, Tim's son, who is responsible for managing all the Humphrys Flag Company operations in a chief operating officer role. At one point he thought he wanted to be a lawyer, until he realized his "affinity for law had to do with political science and history . . . so flags kind of made sense."

If in any way you have lost your sense of American pride, you will no doubt regain it when you step inside Humphrys showroom. There

are American flags everywhere, ranging in sizes from very small to very large. By the entryway you can view a framed picture of the American flag they made for a valued client in 1992, a flag that at one time held the world record for the world's largest flag: It weighed in at over 3,000 pounds and used over 5.5 miles of fabric.

In addition to American flags, you will discover other countries' flags, sports flags, animal flags, and more. Humphrys takes pride in their ability to make any kind of custom flag you desire, and all flags are manufactured at their now 55,000-plus-square-foot facility in Pottstown, Pennsylvania.

Matt described to me the many types of customers at Humphrys: large businesses like professional organizations in the city, art museums, city government organizations, and movie production companies.

There are also some fascinating individuals who help support the store. Did you know there are allegedly competing "flag blocks" in Philadelphia? "Fifth and Delancey was always known as the flag block," Matt tells me. Recently one man decided to compete with this and other flag-filled streets around Philadelphia, so he bought brackets and poles for all his neighbor's houses and paid the cost of installing them to encourage his neighbors to purchase and hang flags from their homes.

Other memorable customers have purchased flags at Humphrys. There's the man working for the Air Force who wanted to bring a flag with him to his new station in Oman. His goal was to take a picture of this flag at the various sites he worked and send these pictures to family back at home, so that everyone in his family could be there in spirit while he was away at war. This way he could share his journey with them.

Sometimes a flag is used as a symbol for personal reasons, sometimes for political reasons. Like when, in 2006, then-president Hugo Chavez of Venezuela decided to change the image of the horse in the national flag. It was a simple change really. On the new flag—among other changes such as adding a star, bow and arrow, and machete—the new image of the horse would reflect the horse galloping to the left instead of to the right. Symbolically, it was a little more complicated; some say it was a metaphor to reflect the president's left-leaning political views.

An unforeseen complication in the flag business is the move to manufacturing flags overseas, where the costs are significantly cheaper.

This is also why Humphrys Flag Company stands apart. So the next time you want a cool American-made product, don't forget about this beautiful flag shop in the middle of a neighborhood where some of the most important moments were made in American history and where the flags are 100 percent "Made in the USA."

IANNELLI'S BAKERY

1155 E. PASSYUNK AVE. • PHILADELPHIA, PA 19147

(215) 468-0720 • IANNELLISBAKERY.COM

Your Own Private Party

*J*t was not the typical run-of-the-mill interview. It's also not your typical run-of-the-mill bakery. It is technically a bakery because you can purchase homemade cannoli, cupcakes, cookies, and other forms of sweets, or preorder some traditional ricotta pies (a kind of Italian cheesecake) for Easter. It also could just as easily be a pizzeria because they're known for their tomato pies and stromboli.

Or, sometimes it even functions as a bring-your-own-bottle restaurant, where you can spend a night out with 10 to 13 of your friends, get served and entertained by your own private chef, and eat until you get "wheelbarrowed out," as Vincent Iannelli, owner of Iannelli's Bakery ("Iannelli's") informs me.

I felt like I could have been "wheelbarrowed out" when I left my interview at Iannelli's on a quiet morning, a day that the bakery was closed. To his credit, he told me to come hungry. I expected possibly a cannoli or a sample of a tomato pie. Instead, I received a full from-scratch breakfast, including eggs made to order, fried potatoes, and toast that was cooked in the brick oven. It was definitely not the typical run-of-the-mill interview. I wouldn't complain if more interviews were like this.

Vince Iannelli is a real character in every sense of the word. He knows he is a character. He prefers it this way. If you choose to come in with a group of friends and rent out the place on a Friday or Saturday night for a "private chef menu," know that Vince will be your private chef. In addition to being able to stuff yourself with all kinds of homemade food as you watch the chef in action, you'll also get free

entertainment. This entertainment will come from the stories that Vince will tell you while you're there, which are undoubtedly funnier and more entertaining than the stories you'd pay to hear at some of the best comedy clubs in the nation.

Inside there's a framed red sign with black bold letters that says, "Very Enforced Policy. Don't Break Balls!" Hope that helps to describe what to expect.

Customers who don't know what to expect will learn their lesson quickly when they speak to Vince. One of Vince's favorite customers—and now a great friend—is a guy by the name of Ross, whose first interaction with Vince was when he called him up on the phone and asked, "You guys got cannolis?"

Vince sarcastically replied "No, we sell Boeing 747s," until he added, "We're a bakery, of course we got ___ cannolis." Insert unsuitable-for-print word in blank space.

Vince runs his business with the objective that all customers should be treated like family. He learned from the best, and that was his own family, including his mom, grandparents, aunts, and uncles, who all owned various businesses in and around the Italian Market. His grandparents Terry and Mirna Iannelli were the original owners of Iannelli's, which they started in 1910, determined, as noted on

Iannelli's website, to "transform the pizza industry with their cheese less, tomato pie pizza."

Vince's career at the bakery started around the time he was 17 years old, but prior to that he worked at other family businesses and with friends at the Italian Market. At 9 years old he was selling eggs on South 9th Street, and if he worked a full Saturday he might even get to take home $15.

The kitchen consumes the bakery's interior, as it should considering all the products and tomato pies they're cranking out of this bakery. The brick oven is the original, as is some of the other equipment, like the antique digital scale they still use. Hanging from the ceiling are racks that store the long wooden pizza trays measuring at least 10

Vintage Spots: Pizza

MARRA'S OF PHILADELPHIA: EST. 1927

A black-tiled building stands out among the other brownstones on Passyunk Avenue. Inside, old wooden booths in a cozy dining room and a view of the brick oven are part of the scene at this traditional pizzeria. For the budget conscious, there's a "Sunset Menu" that's not available only during sunset. For $12.95 you can get a pasta dish with your choice of soup or salad on Tues through Thurs from 11:30 a.m. until 10 p.m. and during lunch hours on Fri and Sat.

1734 E. Passyunk Ave.; (267) 463-9249; marrasone.com

TACCONELLI'S PIZZERIA: EST. 1946

You realize this Port Richmond place—run by the fifth generation of the Tacconelli family—is timeless when you see the way you have to order. The only way to get a pizza is by calling ahead to "reserve your dough." It's cash only with fairly limited dining hours, but customers don't seem to mind all these rules once they get their thin-crust tomato pie in hand.

2604 E. Somerset St.; (215) 425-4983; tacconellispizzeria.com

feet, which are necessary for sliding the pizza in and out of the deep brick oven.

Vince has updated the interior in recent years. The space for customers used to function more like a takeout counter. Today Vince has opened it up, enough to add a few tables where customers can sit inside the bakery to eat. Vince is also making a few changes to the business model. One has been to introduce a shipping service to his customers. He recently shipped two cases of crab gravy to Dallas, Texas.

Their homemade "gravy," or a special kind of homemade tomato sauce, is a customer favorite. Gravy varieties include the family style that is the signature sauce on their tomato pies, diablo style, vodka sauce, crab gravy, spicy crab, and Bolognese.

Vince hopes to transition the bakery to more of a weekend business in the coming years. The reason for this is twofold. One is so he can balance all that intensive labor in the kitchen with something that involves less intensive manual labor; his other job is selling real estate investments. It's also so that Vince can spend time building his business model in other ways, like developing a better web presence and increasing his shipping capacity.

With all this talk of shipping, though, don't forget to visit Iannelli's first and see this beautiful old-school bakery at its home, because it is a destination. You'll be satisfied on your way out whether you come in for a cannoli, a tomato pie, or a six-course dinner.

ISGRO PASTICCERIA

1009 CHRISTIAN ST. • PHILADELPHIA, PA 19147

(215) 923-3092 • BESTCANNOLI.COM

A Baker's Rhythm

*L*ike the famous department stores in big cities around the world, Isgro Pasticceria has its own eye-catching holiday storefront window, yet its window is only the prelude of the beautiful things you'll see. Wait until you see the inside displays and, most importantly, taste them.

In New York City, particularly for the Christmas season, there are lines around the block to admire those gorgeous department-store windows. In Philadelphia, there are lines around the block, too.

There's only one major difference.

The longest lines are not for the holiday windows. They're to get inside this classic, old-fashioned family bakery on Christian Street that becomes overcrowded when there are more than eight customers inside at any given time. The people who wait in these three-hour lines (on average) have already preordered their cannoli, cookies, and other Italian pastry specialties weeks, even months, in advance. Preordering just means you're guaranteed to get your product. No one avoids the lines. It's that good.

Ever hear the adage that you eat with your eyes first? Gus, owner of Isgro Pastries, seems to know there is truth to this saying. *Gorgeous* is one word to describe the bakery delicacies, but even that word doesn't do it justice. Put it this way: You could set up an exhibition for his pastries in the Philadelphia Museum of Art, and they would look like they belong there.

It takes patience to create great art, just as it takes patience to fill a cannoli the best way. Gus's grandmother used to fill the cannoli with

103

a spoon. He continues to follow that tradition because "that's the way it's supposed to be, when every crevice is packed with filling." The only days he strays from this tradition is during the major holidays. If he didn't stray from it, there'd be a line for three days instead of three hours.

Doing things the easy way never really seemed to matter to the Isgro family.

His grandfather Mario Isgro, the original owner, used to own a farm out in Washington Crossing in the early 1900s. On that farm he made his own ricotta, milled his own flour, and pasteurized his own milk. Born in Messina, Italy, Mario was trained in Vienna, Austria, where he was the head chef for a baron, before migrating to the US.

Gus was born into and raised in this business and grew up with the belief that "when you're old enough to put a cherry on a cookie, you're working." Through the years there has been a line of talented bakers, chefs, and leaders in his family who have all contributed to making Isgro Pastries what it is today, like Gus's mom, Mary; his Uncle Sam; and his Uncle Vito—all Mario's children.

His mother used to make lambs out of marzipan that people would buy to put on their tables for Easter. His grandfather built and hand-carved each and every mold. Today they still make a few of those lambs. It's not advertised. It's not listed on their website, Facebook page, or menu. The regular customers know to ask for them.

If you're not a regular customer, don't worry about your opportunity to get equally amazing products that are advertised on their website, such as the cannoli, which come in flavors like ricotta, vanilla, chocolate, mascarpone, and chocolate mousse. Choose from cookies like the pignoli and *pasticcini*. Purchase one of their famous cakes like the ricotta pie (an Easter specialty), the lemon zest pie, or the ricotta rum cake.

If you decide to join the holiday lines at Isgro Pasticceria, you'll get some entertainment in addition to your delicious pastry products. Santa Claus sets up outside and gives out coffee and espresso. There's elves, jugglers, and a regular group of 20 guys who drop by every year on a bus trip and sing to everyone in line. Engagements have happened in this line. Countless memories have been created. Traditions have started here. Gus is humbled by it all, and he explains

Vintage Spot: Bakery

TERMINI BROTHERS BAKERY: EST. 1920S

"Two brothers. One suitcase. One simple dream." This is the story of Termini Brothers' beginning and what has now become a Philadelphia tradition. Similar to Isgro's, Termini Brothers is also famous for its cannoli. In addition to the humble traditional flagship store on 8th Street in South Philly, it now has three other locations, including one in the Reading Terminal Market.

1523 S. 8th St.; (215) 334-1816; termini.com

that he can't fully express in words his gratitude to his customers for remaining loyal to his family's business.

If it's your first visit, don't worry about finding the store. As you get closer, your nose is guaranteed to lead you in the right direction. There's always sweet smells filling up the neighborhood around 10th and Christian Streets.

All the magic happens in the basement. There is no music allowed while they're at work. Gus listens to his own music, that of the "hum of mixers and compressors and fans that are running." When the sounds are different, he knows that there is an issue that needs to be fixed.

The store spans three buildings on Christian Street. It's always physically been based at this location. In the bakery, the marble table, one that Gus's grandfather put in over 100 years ago, still remains. Equipment is replaced as needed, but usually only when absolutely necessary, due to the logistical complications of it all. Every time a new piece of equipment is installed, riggers have to be on-site with a crane, where the front window is first removed and then equipment is dropped into the basement.

With all the building's challenges, Gus has thought about moving, but he knows he can't leave the history of this store, the strong weight of 110 years of memories that have passed through this building that seems to be alive. Across from him, his longtime manager Denise smiles. She agrees. She's felt it and seen it herself. Sometimes the big calculators start working by themselves at random times throughout the day. They tried moving them around the room, even buying new ones, but nothing changed. They still work on their own. "There is a life, a rhythm that's here," Gus confirms.

JOE'S STEAKS & SODA SHOP

6030 TORRESDALE AVE. • PHILADELPHIA, PA 19135

(215) 535-9405 • JOESSTEAKS.COM

Shakin' It Up

J t could be a scene from any classic 1950s Hollywood movie, or maybe from the TV series *Happy Days*. An old dial pay phone hangs from the entrance door. The grill, well-used from years of cooking cheesesteaks, is front and center, granting people who pass by from the outside the temptation to see and smell all the deliciousness inside. Seating choices range from a small bar counter with five silver barstools covered with a drab, out-of-date-but-full-of-character brown padding to unmovable 1950s wooden booths. There are the original tin ceilings, a soda fountain, and individual (but no longer functioning) jukeboxes at every booth. All of this surrounds you as you feast on—you guessed it—a homemade steak and soda at Joe's Steak & Soda Shop.

You could also choose a milk shake as your beverage of choice. Choose from traditional flavors like vanilla, chocolate, or mint chocolate chip, or try out the seasonal menu that includes a few new shakes every month. Past flavors have included Apple Pie for Thanksgiving, Orange Creamsicle for the summer, or the Candy Corn milkshake for Halloween.

When the shop was established in 1949, there was not this much diversity in the menu selection. Nor was there much diversity in the neighborhood, which is clear from the original name: Chink's Steaks. It was owned by a Caucasian man named Sam Sherman, nicknamed "Chink" because of his almond-shaped eyes. Sounds offensive nowadays, but in the 1940s and '50s it didn't carry quite the weight it does today. Or the consequences.

Current owner Joe Groh purchased the shop officially in 1999 a few years after Chink passed away, but he has been working at the shop since 1979, where his first task was peeling the onions in the basement. Over the years, he did everything, from chopping the steak to mopping and cleaning the entire shop down and removing the remnants of all the cheesesteaks consumed in the place on a daily basis.

When he bought the place he kept the name because it was tradition. He also wanted to honor the wishes of some of the regular customers who were opposed to any kind of change, big or small.

For most business owners there comes a time when change is needed. Because without change, you may not be able to grow or to maintain your successful business operation. You may not even be able to survive.

Joe was one of those business owners. He knew his time had come, especially because he couldn't grow his business without a new name. No one would approve a business in the 21st century with the name "Chink's." So in 2013, he changed the name.

Before the official name change, souvenir shirts were a huge seller. Sometimes he sold 25 Chink's T-shirts a day. After the name change, there were bad times, and even more "bad badgering," as

Joe described to me. Badgering that came from the customers, like an old lady who came in, ordered a sandwich, then called the waitress over and complained, "I can't do it. It's not a Chink's sandwich." She walked out, leaving it untouched.

Or from online trolls who plastered bad comments on social media pages and on website review pages. All of this badgering was the result of Joe changing only two things: the store's name and the sign outside. Inside you could sit in the same booths from the 1950s. You could eat the same exact cheesesteak. You could order it from the same staff who'd been working there when it was called Chink's. Did you ever hear the song titled "People Are Crazy"?

Sometimes people are crazy. It's no surprise that you can't please every customer. This badgering did not ruin Joe's business nor stop him from recently making a few more changes to add variety to his menu selection, thereby pleasing a few of his new customers. Keep the same products but adapt to the times.

Joe credits his manager Stefani for contributing her ideas and for her leadership in implementing some significant changes. Today that menu includes fries and a choice of a chicken sandwich (or chicken cheesesteak sandwich). There are also more cheese choices. In the past it was American or American. Now you can get American and Cheez Whiz.

With the new name, Joe's business can expand as planned. Joe's Steaks has recently opened a new location in Fishtown, with more seating inside, an area for outside seating, and late-night hours to cater to the neighborhood. His son, Patrick, and manager, Stefani, will be on-site regularly at that location, while he runs the operations at his original shop.

The original shop, with seating for approximately 30 customers, is a hidden treasure in the middle of Northeast Philadelphia. Unlike many of the cheesesteak shops in other parts of Philadelphia, this one actually lets you sit down inside and relax.

For those travelers passing through, it's a convenient location, with close proximity to the major highway, I-95, one of the main interstates running through the East Coast of the US. Nothing better than a cheesesteak and shake or soda break before you continue your journey.

JOHN'S ROAST PORK

14 E. SNYDER AVE. • PHILADELPHIA, PA 19148

(215) 463-1951 • JOHNSROASTPORK.COM

Savor Every Second

The image of the happy pig, getting ready to sit down for dinner, is the iconic mascot on the otherwise plain cinder-block building. The same pig picture is displayed on the sign at the top of the building and from every angle along the building's sides.

Today they should consider adding a cow next to the pig. That might sound ridiculous at a place called John's Roast Pork, but those who know John's Roast Pork also know that they make some amazing beef, too.

Still, the pig does reflect its beginnings, focused solely on the pork, where the secret recipe was invented in a garage. The garage then evolved into a humble wooden shack along Snyder Avenue, a shack with just two main products: roast pork and meatballs. In 1967, the shack was torn down and a new cinder-block building was built, still an unassuming, simple, no-frills building, with no indoor seating but some outside picnic tables. This is the building you still see today.

In prior years, John's Roast Pork was a breakfast and lunch stop only, a place to feed the hungry construction workers and dockworkers in South Philly, particularly special for those workers who wanted to enjoy a robust breakfast before a day of hard physical labor. An average breakfast sandwich is robust, with three eggs, three pieces of cheese, and seven pieces of bacon. A robust breakfast goes hand in hand with a robust lunch. Look at the steak sandwich to align your expectations. It is stacked with 12 ounces of beef.

Today the neighborhood that used to shut down by midafternoon has developed. A strip of shopping plazas line Snyder Avenue.

Clothing chains, home improvement stores, furniture stores, and grocery stores have moved in nearby, prompting a change to John's opening hours that will now make it a midafternoon and early-dinner stop.

Along with the neighborhood, the business has transformed. It's normal to expect that a family business often transforms as it is passed down from generation to generation. There's major pressure that comes along with a legacy that another family member has built. Sometimes the next generation isn't passionate about inheriting that legacy. Sometimes they are. John Bucci Jr., current owner of John's Roast Pork, understands both sides. In past years his passion for the business was partially lost.

He eventually found it again about four or five years ago, around the exact same time he got his second chance at life.

At one point in that first phase of his life, John Jr. was on his way toward a career as a sports psychologist. He was attending college at St. Joseph's University until family duty called, and he left to help his mom continue the family business when his father, John Sr., developed health problems and, soon after, passed away in 1991.

John Jr. has a knack for making sandwiches, beginning with the pork, which he made according to his grandmother's famous recipe. His next contribution was making a few tweaks to improve the cheesesteak that was on their menu. Just recently, he's created a new version of the roast beef sandwich.

All of this care that John and his family put into the sandwich preparation eventually paid off and brought John attention beyond the locals in South Philly, beginning with a *Philadelphia Inquirer* article written by the restaurant critic Craig LaBan in 2000. Soon after, in 2002, Craig LaBan and four teenagers drove 111 miles to 23 different restaurants in search of the best cheesesteak sandwich, and named John's Roast Pork as the winner. To this day, John Jr. still credits Craig LaBan as the guy who put John's Roast Pork on the map.

Craig LaBan continued to follow John's story when it became a more personal story, a story less about the business and more about John's battle with leukemia, a battle that officially began in 2006 when he received the diagnosis. His chances were small. Without a bone marrow transplant, he would die, and even with a donor match, his chances for long-term success were still about 50 percent. In 2008, they found a donor, and John Jr. had the bone marrow transplant. During that long recovery period, other family members, like his niece Bethany and his wife, Vickie, stepped in to run the business, while he fought for a successful recovery.

John won the fight, and the wall art inside this humble cinderblock building helps tell the whole story today. There's a wedding picture of John Sr. and Vonda serving pork at their own wedding reception, and a similar picture next to it of John Jr. and Vickie, who re-created that same scene at their own wedding. There are countless articles written about them, praising their business and their food. There are honors they have received, awards they have been nominated for, and contests they've won.

John Jr.'s knack for making sandwiches didn't carry over to the same knack with servicing and appreciating the customers. John Jr. recalls a time when he received a bad review in a local press article. Comparing him with the character of the Soup Nazi in the popular TV show *Seinfeld,* they called John Jr. the "Pork Nazi." He admits his embarrassment when he thinks about his attitude before his leukemia diagnosis. You would never believe those stories when you meet John today.

His happiness is infectious. Just like his sandwiches.

JOHN'S WATER ICE

701 CHRISTIAN ST. • PHILADELPHIA, PA 19147

(215) 925-6955 • JOHNSWATERICE.COM

Simply Icy

No need to overthink anything. Sometimes the simple way is the best way. You might be programmed to think differently after years of education. Countless professors and business executives preach that you have to make changes for your business to survive and adapt to the changing times. I challenge anyone with this belief to look at the John's Water Ice operation.

I guarantee it'll change your views on change.

The original layout, a modest brick building, hasn't changed. Half of the building is used for the water-ice operation. The other half is used for another Cardullo family business, a business that provides home heating and air-conditioning services. There are no customer seats inside or outside. There never have been seats from the beginning, though you're welcome to sit on the curbside.

The main ingredients haven't changed. It's the old tried-and-true recipe of fruit plus sugar plus water. Real fruit. No preservatives.

The family in charge of the operation hasn't changed either. John Cardullo started the business in 1945, around the same time he started others, like the heating and air-conditioning business next door. When he passed away, his sons took over the businesses he started. Today, the businesses are all still family owned and operated. They have been divided up among family members. Anthony Cardullo, the third generation, has resumed ownership of the water-ice business while his cousins run the heating and air-conditioning business next door.

That's not to say there haven't been a few changes along the way.

The neighborhood around this area of Philadelphia changed . . . somewhat. Years ago, in an article in *USA Today*, John's gained media attention when it was mentioned in an article entitled "10 Great Places to Discover Italy in America." For a long time this neighborhood was all Italian Americans. It's now more of a cultural mix. But John's is still centrally located near all of the Italian family-owned businesses at the Italian Market, a short five-block walk away.

Flavors have changed . . . gradually. What started as two flavors—cherry and lemon—evolved into two more flavors, chocolate and pineapple. Almost 45 years later a few more flavors were added to incorporate some weekend specials. Flavors like strawberry, piña colada, cantaloupe, banana, and mango are among the specials you might see today. Some days you might have a selection of four flavors. Other days you might be fortunate to see that selection increase to seven flavors.

Customers have changed. Celebrities have stopped by from time to time. Professional football players. Actors. Even President Obama, who stopped by for a water ice in 2011 during a quick visit to Philadelphia.

Machines have changed . . . also very gradually over time. In the beginning, it was a hand-cranking operation. By the 1960s it was slightly more advanced—there was a motor in place of the arm motion.

I commented on the amount of arm strength you must have needed to have to keep this business going day after day. Since the late 1960s automatic machines have been used. Anthony seems rather happy that he never had to operate the machines the "old-school" way. "I'm the smallest one in this family," he told me. "My father and uncle were animals . . . all really big. One uncle was six feet, four inches tall and weighed 350 pounds." Okay, that is big, though the average person would never, ever describe Anthony as small. He's six feet tall and 200 pounds.

Today there are four machines. The "newest" machine, installed 16 years ago, cranks out 40 quarts of water ice in approximately 12 minutes. The older ones crank out the same 40 quarts in almost double that amount of time.

If all machines lasted as long as water-ice machines, I think we'd all be a lot happier, or at the very least there'd be a lot less complaining among homeowners about unexpected expenses or replacements.

Dishwashers last on average about 10 years. Refrigerators last on average 15 to 20 years. John's is still using one machine that's over 40 years old.

Along with cheesesteaks and soft pretzels, the city of Philadelphia is well known for its water ice. That has resulted in countless competitions over which establishment has the best water ice, and John's has regularly been on the top of the lists.

The texture of their ice is balanced and smooth. Just as balanced and smooth as the entire operation, with a season that starts around April 1 and continues until September 22. Employees are comprised of family members and friends. One person works the machine, two people work the front window. Ice is produced continually throughout the day as supply decreases. This is the same way it's been done for years and years, with daily operating hours until 10 p.m. every night.

These hours seem to suit Anthony Cardullo. When John's Water Ice closes for the season, he goes to work at a traditional Italian restaurant nearby, the Saloon, another great family-run place with good people and scrumptious food. I asked what he'd want to do if he weren't in the ice business. His answer comes easy. "Probably work in the restaurant business." It's that simple.

JOSEPH FOX BOOKSHOP

1724 SANSOM ST. • PHILADELPHIA, PA 19103

(215) 563-4184 • FOXBOOKSHOP.COM

Building a Story

One of its original specialties was architecture. The kinds of books that were eye-catching and showy and didn't fit perfectly in a standard-size bookshelf made for standard-style book sizes for the standard kind of fiction books.

Nothing about the Joseph Fox Bookshop has ever been "standard."

Originally it was smaller than standard, a bookstore that opened up in 1951 in a downstairs basement of a building. The 1,200-square-foot interior space is limited, but the book selection is vast. There are architectural titles like *Sensing Spaces, A Field Guide to American Houses, Designing Legends*, and *The House with Sixteen Handmade Doors*. Keep searching and you might come across diverse interest books labeled *My Little Book of Chinese Words*, or *Comics: A Global History, 1968 to the Present*. Or you might focus on a massive book twice the size of other books entitled *The Book of Funghi: A Life-Size Guide to Six Hundred Species from around the World*.

Many bookstores have collections devoted to the *New York Times* bestseller list, but Joseph Fox Bookshop has a collection devoted to the *New York Times Book Review* instead. Two very different types of lists for anyone who knows a thing or two about books.

Head to the back of the store and you'll see a cute, tucked-in children's book section. Other focuses include emphases on book categories like poetry, music, art, and serious nonfiction.

This story, however, isn't all about the books. It's about the people who have been spending their lives keeping this independent bookstore in business since 1951 . . . and it's still going.

Like Joseph M. Fox, namesake of the store, who started the store on a shoestring budget because he had a passion for books. He never graduated from high school, but he always had a driving force to read more and see more. He served in the Army Air Corps during World War II, and while in Guam, he helped to build a library.

Or Joseph's wife, who regularly worked 60 hours a week at the bookstore through the age of 87.

Then there's another man involved in this business, one of the major characters in this story, named Michael Fox. Michael is the current owner and has been the majority shareholder since 2001. Before he was the majority shareholder, he was highly involved in all aspects of the business, running it like his own while his father was battling Alzheimer's. Before he was involved in all aspects of the business, he was packing and unpacking books, "an art form in itself," as Michael Fox relayed to me while cracking a smile. The store has existed since Michael Fox was born.

Next there is someone who plays the dynamic character role. Dynamic characters are ones that go through some kind of change

Vintage Spot: Bookstore
GIOVANNI'S ROOM: EST. 1973

It made a name for itself as the "oldest and best gay and lesbian bookstore in the country" since its opening in what is now known as the "gayborhood" section of Center City, filled with rainbow flags and some popular well-established gay bars and nightclubs. Recently saved from closing by the Philly AIDS Thrift organization, it's now renamed Philly AIDS Thrift @ Giovanni's Room, and it's still the place to go for service and an amazing selection and database of gay and lesbian specialty titles.

345 S. 12th St.; (215) 923-2960; queerbooks.com

over the course of the book, and that's definitely Judi Fox, Michael's wife, who, as Michael shares with me, "has taken a bigger and bigger role" in the business.

There are lots of other characters that are important to this story, including the four full-time employees—Kate, Mandy, Mary, and Joe—who are experts on books. They are ready to help any customer find that rare, hard-to-find book. The bookstore prides itself on its special ordering service. The staff is ready to solve the vaguest kinds of requests: "I don't know the exact title or the author, but it was written in the last year, and it has the word *power* somewhere in the title."

Every single character at Joseph Fox Bookshop plays multiple roles and fulfills their part in keeping the operation running day after day. That may be finding solutions for the customers who ask seemingly impossible questions to answer.

Or organizing big author events, such as the time the bookshop hosted David Sedaris at the store and closed off the street outside the library to accommodate the crowds of people who attended the event.

Or organizing and running other types of literary events through their partnering relationship with the Free Library of Philadelphia (freelibrary.org), chartered in 1891 as a "general library, which shall be free to all." Recent author events featured people including David Mitchell, Tavis Smiley, and Henry Kissinger.

So my advice is to look past the front cover of this book. On the cover you might only see a narrow building squeezed in between fancy Rittenhouse Square hotels and clothing stores. You might see one modest window showcasing some books and a name, Joseph Fox, in italics, followed by the word *bookstore*.

Take the advice of a man named Michael, who has worked hard to carry on the work that his father began, when he says, "Independent bookstores are fundamental to the character of the US."

LUCIO MANCUSO & SON

1902 E. PASSYUNK AVE. • PHILADELPHIA, PA 19148

(215) 389-1817 • MANCUSOSCHEESE.COM

A Taste of Italy

*J*t was common to get orders for portion sizes of 5 and 10 pounds. Families were larger, and many women who lived in the neighborhood were homemakers who were used to cooking for a family of 5 to 10 people every night. Those families knew how to use soft and creamy cheeses to satisfy even the fussiest person in their family. In those years home-cooked meals were more commonplace. Eating out was only for a special occasion.

Eating out today is now for any occasion. There are at least "30 restaurants on East Passyunk from McKean to Dickinson," Philip Mancuso, owner of Lucio Mancuso & Son, tells me. East Passyunk Avenue has evolved over the years and is now a trendy, transformed Philadelphia street often referred to by food enthusiasts as "restaurant row." Times have changed. Businesses have closed and new businesses have been established. But amid all that change, there's one shop named Lucio Mancuso & Son that has stayed true to its roots. This shop has found a way to adapt and to survive in an environment very different from its original environment and the predominant culture of Italian Americans who lived in that environment. What's incredible, and enduring, is that this store has largely remained the same even when all the people and customers around it have changed.

This shop is all that Philip Massimo Mancuso has ever known. He was born and raised in South Philly. The cheese shop at 1902 E. Passyunk Ave. opened in 1940. His father, Lucio, was the original owner, who opened the cheese shop when Philip was 5 years old. You do the math. Philip Mancuso has spent a long time at the cheese shop.

Philip remembers watching his father work from an early age. His childhood toys weren't from a toy store. They were the big broom used to sweep the floors or the canned goods that he would often rearrange to make into his own designs.

Philip has been running the store officially since his father passed away in 1971, spending at least 12 hours there every day. I asked him if he ever takes a vacation. His response was "every night." That pretty much explains his work ethic.

He still makes homemade ricotta and mozzarella as he's always done from old-fashioned vats. The production is just a little smaller now than it used to be. People aren't ordering in 10-pound portions anymore to feed their big, growing families.

Inside, the store is stuffed to the brim with Italian import products. The store was once a little smaller. There used to be an upstairs apartment that was turned into a storage facility in the 1950s and 1960s. There was a large renovation and remodeling in the late 1950s. Most of the equipment still there today is from that remodeling date—around 1958—like the glass refrigerators behind the counter that hold various specialty cheeses and meats.

Purchase some handmade ricotta to make lasagna, ravioli, cannoli, or maybe a cheesecake. Choose from other cheeses like mozzarella, sharp provolone, and Parmagiano Reggiano. Or dried meats, olives. Olive oils, vinegars, pastas. Espresso and cappuccino. Water ice.

If you're new to the neighborhood and haven't yet entered, the window display will surely be the best hint of what you can find inside, stacked with products like Nutella, Ferrara Italian confectionary chocolates, and Roman-style artichokes. They now make specialty gift baskets that are customized according to your desires. If you can't find the product you want, just ask. Chances are Philip Mancuso will try to get it for you. As times have changed, the shop has adapted with the customers. The staff try to get what people are asking for and remain competitive with pricing.

It's your local neighborhood shop. Italian focused. But still the shop that's meant to give you your favorite product, that helps conjure a sense of home, at a good price.

Today Philip's son, Philip Joseph, also has a hand in running the shop. He's learned from his father, the same way that his father learned from his grandfather.

When I left, I spent some time outside the store taking a few pictures and looking at its distinct spot in this neighborhood. It was a quiet midweek day in South Philly. But for a second it could have been Sicily. It was like an old painting, a beautiful, traditional work of art. Something tells me a picture like this was already been painted. If not, it should be.

There was Philip Massimo Mancuso, who had resumed his spot on the bench outside the store. He was wearing his baseball cap splashed with the bold lettering "Italia Roma" next to a picture of the Italian flag. He was wearing his long apron, his standard uniform, which undoubtedly hasn't changed much since 1940. He was sitting next to the old sign lit up in green and blue reading "Mancuso Cheese Product" beside the shop where he's spent the majority of his life so far. Where he will undoubtedly spend the rest of his life, waiting for his next customer to arrive.

MCGILLIN'S OLDE ALE HOUSE

1310 DRURY ST. • PHILADELPHIA, PA 19107

(215) 735-5562 • MCGILLINS.COM

A Good Olde Time

*O*nce you get in, it's often hard to get out. That's quite possibly true for some of McGillin's Olde Ale House guests. It's also true for the McGillin's owners, Chris and Mary Ellen Mullins, and probably for their son, Christopher Jr., relative to their careers within the restaurant business. Most of the time, though, this is a good thing. The restaurant business is always an interesting one.

There are certain restaurants and bars you step into where you know you have to be a certain type of person. Like the one that used to be your favorite hangout in a past life. You're so excited to go back and relive all the fun you had there, until you get inside and realize that everyone is still the same age that you were in that past life. You've become the oldest one.

There are bars that are tourist bars that the locals stay away from, and there are bars that are locals-only bars that the tourists stay away from.

Then there's McGillin's. Let's just say there are a few types of people who might fit in at this establishment:

History buffs, including history majors, history teachers, or anyone at all who has the slightest appreciation of old things. According to its official website, McGillin's is the "oldest continuously operating tavern in Philadelphia." The place opened when James Buchanan was the president of the US. He was the 15th president. Abraham Lincoln wasn't even in office yet. When the tiled floors and swinging windows were added, the same ones that still exist today, Theodore Roosevelt

was president. Twenty-nine presidents' terms have come and gone, and McGillin's is still going strong.

Tourists who will only go to the highest ranked or "must-see" spots. McGillin's has been named on a few media lists over the years, including "Top 10 Irish Pubs in the US" (Fox News, March 2013 and 2014), "Most Authentic Irish Pubs in America" (*USA Today* and Huffington Post, March 2013), "One of 14 Coolest Bars in the US" (*Gourmet*, 2008). You can count on McGillin's Olde Ale House to be named in your Philadelphia tourist guide.

Those who love a good story. The original bar owner, an Irish immigrant named William McGillin, raised his 13 children in the upstairs room above the bar. Since the bar's opening, only two families have ever been involved in the ownership of the business.

Those who will only go out if there's a bargain or special. McGillin's continues to have specials every single day of the week. Pitcher specials, Bloody Mary specials, 35-cent wing nights, $6 meals.

Those who love craft beer. When Chris and Mary Ellen took over the business in 1993, there were five beers on tap. Today that list has expanded to over 40 tap lines and at least 30 different brands on draft at any given time. They even have their own regular house beers, a lager and an ale brewed especially for McGillin's by Stoudts Brewing Company in Adamstown, Pennsylvania. For McGillin's 150th anniversary party back in 2010, Stoudt's brewed them another special—a McGillin's 1860 IPA.

Locals who want to see a friendly face and enjoy some comfort foods. Like any great bar, McGillin's has its share of regular customers who have their go-to barstool and their go-to food order. Food selections include traditional bar food like buffalo wings, fries, nachos, and shrimp, but McGillin's takes it up a notch by offering more choices and spicing up the food. Fries can be spiced up with Old Bay Seasoning or cheesed up with cheddar. Or you can go for the Tex-Mex fries, spicy batter-dipped curly fries smothered with cheeses, jalapeño peppers, salsa, and sour cream. There's a selection of sandwiches, steaks, seafood, salads, and even a traditional Irish shepherd's pie. A food menu to go with the atmosphere. Something for everyone.

Point is, you'll fit in, regardless of your age, weight, sexual preference, height, or local status. As long as you're up for a fun day or night out. As Chris expresses it, "I hate using a cliché about the idea that McGillin's is like the *Cheers* bar, but . . ."

The neighborhood around McGillin's has changed over the years, considering this bar was here before the Philadelphia City Hall building was built. At one time this neighborhood was predominantly filled with banking and finance offices; then when the financial centers moved west in the city, it became an attractive spot for department stores, shopping, and other tourist sites.

Considering all the recent awards, media attention, and prestige around McGillin's, you'd expect the atmosphere might change along with the neighborhood. The best part is that it hasn't. It's still a neighborhood bar.

The bar business is a tough one, especially knowing how to maintain that neighborhood bar for over 150 years. Co-owner Chris Mullins began his bar and restaurant career at 10 years old. When a career officially starts by dishing up 500 plates of peas for an Irish wedding, it can only go up from there. That's how it worked for Chris. His father was a chef, so Chris, by default, assumed various restaurant roles throughout the years on Cape Cod. Busboy, dishwasher, cook, waiter. You name it, Chris probably did it.

Mary Ellen's father, Henry, originally bought McGillin's in 1958, so she's also quite the expert in the restaurant business. Chris Jr. was raised in the restaurant business much the same way his own parents were, and now he has decided to follow in his parents' footsteps, continuing the McGillin's legacy.

They're running a serious business. With around 60 to 65 employees, a space of over 2,800 square feet between the two floors, and a great location in the middle of Center City, they're not only surviving, they're flourishing.

MCMENAMIN'S TAVERN

7170 GERMANTOWN AVE. • PHILADELPHIA, PA 19119

(215) 247-9920

Rebirth of the Neighborhood Bar

*I*t's funny how life works out sometimes. No one forced him to get into the bar business. His father actually pushed him to stay away from it. Far, far away.

Maybe it was because the bar had unfortunately turned into a hub for regulars who were known to drink a few too many shots. Or get into brawls. Or, in addition to alcohol, use a few stronger mind-enhancing substances. Maybe it was because of the neighborhood, which at one point was the hub for those types of people.

Regardless of what it was, P. J. McMenamin did the opposite. He grew nearer and closer to the business. So close that after his father passed away, he decided, at 21 years old, that he'd run the bar. At first just to pay off previous family debts from the business. Then it turned into something more substantial. He used his savings to renovate the place. His grandfather, the original owner of the bar, is probably proud of this, probably watching him from above. If anything, he's literally watching him from above. His portrait hangs from the wall at the center of the bar.

P. J.'s grandfather was Patrick McMenamin, who started out as a caretaker for a big estate in Chestnut Hill, then in 1936 purchased a bar for $500, and for two years he made payments until he fulfilled the lease agreement. In 1939 he moved the bar to the current location, where it's been ever since. It was known as Mount Airy Tavern.

It started as a shot-and-beer place. A bar for the men in front and the women in the back, where there was a separate ladies' entrance. A place for shift workers who worked from midnight until seven or eight in the morning and then stopped by the bar. P. J.'s grandmother used to open up the bar at 7 a.m. and work until 12 p.m., and then her husband would take over, working from 12 p.m. until 2 a.m. This is the routine they assumed six days a week for most of their lives.

By 1942 P. J.'s grandparents bought the whole building and lived above the bar. When other family members would visit the bar, they'd also stay the night. Ten people to a room on weekend nights were not uncommon. When P. J.'s father, Charlie, took over, it was still a shot-and-beer venue. By the time P. J. took over in 1989, there were a few menu items like hot dogs and meatball sandwiches. Yet it was not a place to go out for dinner. It was primarily a place to drink and occasionally order food when you realized you were hungry or you wanted to absorb some of the alcohol you just drank.

By the early to mid-1990s, food began to play a larger part in the business. P. J.'s mom was doing a lot of the cooking and making everything from hot roast beef sandwiches to meatballs to fresh homemade soups. By 1997 P. J. busted a hole in the back wall and added a real kitchen, eliminating the makeshift kitchen setup originally behind the bar.

Vintage Spot: Bar
GREY LODGE PUB: EST. 1950

A Northeast Philly neighborhood bar in the community of Mayfair since 1950, this bar has some of the great original features and casual vibe that come along with a loyal neighborhood following. Best change, though, since the current owner, known only by his nickname, "Scoats," took over in 1994, is the beer; in recent years they've won numerous prestigious awards for their impressive selection. Visit for their cool events like Festivus, Friday the Firkenteenth, or Groundhog Day.
6235 Frankford Ave. (215) 856-3591; greylodge.com

Prior to busting a hole in the back wall, he also made some other much-needed renovations. He replaced the outdated 1950s bar made out of glass blocks with a Formica top and put in the wood bar they still have today. He took a wall down to open up the 1,000-square-foot room.

Another major turning point was the change in beer. As early as 1994, P. J. began putting craft beer from microbreweries on tap, beginning with a pilsner from Stoudts Brewing Company in Adamstown.

Shortly after, along with the improvements to the food menu and the beer menu, the neighborhood began to improve. Bicycle police started patrolling Mount Airy, a successful tactic because they'd be able to sneak up on the delinquents using a very quiet means of transportation .

McMenamin's Tavern, though a fixture in the neighborhood from the '30s on, also sneaked up in the ranks of best bars within the city of Philadelphia. With 17 beers on tap, a consistent, quality bar-food menu, and its reputation for high-quality staff (Paul, one of the bartenders, has now been at McMenamin's since about 1997), it turned into an iconic spot. It has been one of the regular bars on the *Philadelphia* magazine's "Foobooz 50 Best Bars of Philadelphia" list on multiple occasions. Today it is the place that you can go to three or four nights every week and never get tired of the great company and scene.

During my visit and after my meeting with P. J., I stopped to look around. It was the start of a midweek happy hour. The song "Tiny Dancer" by Elton John was playing. A few regulars ordered a beer at the bar. All I wanted to do was to join them, order a beer and a roast beef sandwich, and settle in for the night. Unfortunately, work called, but it's one of those places.

You would never guess that it all started with a 21-year-old kid who knew nothing about the bar business. A kid who was saving up, working in construction, and going to night school for marketing with a plan to use his savings and move to New Orleans. Instead he bought a bar, renovated it, and turned it into a quintessential neighborhood pub. Often on weeknight evenings when he's not officially working, P. J., his wife, and two daughters will stop by McMenamin's for dinner. He summed it up simply: "I love my job. I get to drink beer every day."

MCNALLY'S TAVERN

8634 GERMANTOWN AVE. • PHILADELPHIA, PA 19118

(215) 247-9736 • MCNALLYSTAVERN.COM

A Tavern and a Trolley

It was a comfy place to eat and relax for the workers on break who operated one of the world's longest streetcar routes between South Philadelphia and Chestnut Hill. That was how McNally's Quick Lunch began in 1921. By 1927, the business grew, so Rose and Hugh McNally purchased a building across the street and turned it into a tavern. Times have changed since then. The streetcar stopped running in the early 1990s, but McNally's is cruising on, still a comfy, relaxing, go-to spot where Rose's great-granddaughters, Anne and Meg, currently run the operation.

As new generations enter the family business, new ideas are generated about the way the business should be run. Compromises have to be made. At first those compromises came in the form of a phone and a clock.

The phone was a big deal when it arrived in the late 1950s. It took years of persuasion before a pay phone was installed, and more persuasion until another type of phone was installed. Well, half of a phone in theory. Incoming calls, no outgoing calls. These were big compromises.

The clock was another negotiation. Anne's grandfather Hugh hated the idea of a clock because he didn't want people to know how long they had spent at the bar. Good reason. So when they did ultimately hang a clock, it was an antique one that had to be wound manually.

After Prohibition, McNally's functioned mainly as a beer-and-shots kind of business. The bar was open from 6 a.m. until 11 p.m. Although 6 a.m. now seems like a crazy time to order a beer and a shot, it worked for the large number of shift workers who would finish work, have a beer, and go back home and to bed at 10 a.m. to get ready for their next night of work.

By the 1960s business was slowing down as the community around Chestnut Hill changed, and Hugh knew it was time to make a few of his own changes.

One of those changes was to revamp the food menu. This was around the time Hugh added the Schmitter sandwich. It was called the Schmitter because the sandwich would be paired with a Schmidt's beer. Regularly referred to as Philadelphia's "Big League sandwich," this now-famous creation is served at major-league venues such as Citizens Bank Park and Lincoln Financial Field. It takes the idea of a Philly cheesesteak to a whole new level. Inside are the basic ingredients of a cheesesteak—fried onions, steak, and cheese. Then more layers are added, more cheese, grilled salami, and tomatoes, all packed and piled inside a Kaiser roll. You can purchase your own T-shirt at the bar that explains it more clearly. It breaks down the sandwich in chart form, the same way a student in school views charts of the human body.

Another of those changes was a much needed transformation of the customer base, when McNally's transformed from a men-only establishment to one serving both women and men.

A final change was to revamp the place. Bathrooms were moved downstairs to accommodate more space and seating; otherwise everything's in place. You'll still find the same narrow bar, with room for about 10 barstools. Another row of approximately five or six tables decorated with flowered tablecloths. You'll see pewter mugs engraved with the McNally's family crest hanging from the ceiling and on the wall behind the bar, part of a mug club that started in the '60s. Unfortunately many of those mugs are no longer in use—part of the normal passing of time that can only exist with a place that has been around this long.

It's a dark kind of place with dark wood walls and beams and dim fluorescent lighting. You may occasionally get some sunlight peeking in, if the front door is open to Germantown Avenue.

When Anne began taking a larger role in the business in the 1980s, eventually becoming an owner in the business in 1994, she had to negotiate with the family to make changes, the same way her father negotiated with his parents about the clock and phone many years earlier.

Her requests were simple enough. One was to create a printed food menu. The other was to create an actual physical handwritten check to provide to customers. Not surprisingly, this method worked better than the honor system, when the customers and bartenders would work together to figure out the total bill. It could get rather complicated based on the length of their stay and number of drinks they ordered.

Because of its long history as a bar and restaurant, there's no shortage of great stories about the customers who've frequented the place. One group of customers treated McNally's as their second home. Jack was one of them. His mail was often sent to McNally's, and he'd get his own phone calls there, too. Family would know to call him there when they wanted to talk to him. When he passed away, there was a small, personal funeral service at the bar. It seemed fitting. Another member of that same group has a plaque named after him, still hanging inside the bar today. The plaque says "Jerry's Corner."

Anne described it in the best possible way. "If these walls could talk . . ." She's right. Great stories have been told in this bar. Great moments that have now become stories have transpired in this bar. Whether or not you're a newcomer or a regular, you can't help feeling the weight of all this great history as you sit inside McNally's Tavern.

THE MERMAID INN

7673 GERMANTOWN AVE. • PHILADELPHIA, PA 19118
(215) 247-9797 • THEMERMAIDINN.NET

Fiddlers on Germantown Avenue

Catchy, engaging fiddle tunes reverberated through the room, so catchy that they would surely be reverberating through my head for the following days and weeks to come.

Twenty chairs in the main bar room formed a circle, where the musicians sat, playing their guitars, banjos, and fiddles in unison.

You could tell the musicians had seen and done this all before. There was a smooth, organized rhythm to the entire night, beginning with the way they filtered into the bar. One by one they entered, followed by a brief interlude of setting up, opening their instrument cases, waving hello to the others, maybe purchasing a drink at the bar.

Then the music filled the room.

This was the Old Time Jam session, one of the recurring events at the Mermaid Inn. Held once per month, some musicians come from a mile away, others come from 50 miles away or more. They all come with one purpose in mind: the music.

They come for the music and stay for the scene, a scene that will change every night based on the type of show that's taking place. Recurring events at the Mermaid Inn include open mike nights, an Irish *seisiún* (or session), and singer/songwriter performances. On weekends there's bands playing music styles that include acoustic deadgrass, rockin' blues, and gypsy jazz.

Events usually begin at nine o'clock in the evening. This one, fittingly, began an hour earlier at eight. It was an "old-time" jam, after all.

What won't change is the venue where the music is played: a dark, historic, haunted, mesmerizing inn turned bar, full of character. Throughout the room there are wide stained-glass windows, most with a hand-painted picture of a mermaid in the center. In the center of one of the windows is a plaque, reading "Welcome to the Historic Mermaid Inn, Established 1734." For hundreds of years, the Mermaid Inn was an inn and a hotel, thought to be a stagecoach stop on the way to Valley Forge. It wasn't until around 1919 that it became a bar. Some records suggest that the old Mermaid Hotel was demolished around 1913 to accommodate a new road passing through the Chestnut Hill community (Keels and Jarvis 2002).

Antique chandeliers hang above the rich wood bar, the original bar from the early 20th century. Two other rooms adjacent to the main bar area offer even more intimate surroundings, making it a convenient place to settle in when you want to have intimate conversations with your friends or a loved one, where you can listen to the entertainment in the next room as background music.

A small locally sourced food menu includes soups, sandwiches, and a few other bar snacks.

A full bar, cash only, presents all the regular options you'd expect. There are Italian and French wines, a few beer options on draft, and a particularly impressive list of about 10 Belgian beers. Choose from a selection of "spirits"—in quotation marks because, as Joanne Mekis, co-owner of the Mermaid Inn, explains, spirits don't just mean the drinks at this place.

Joanne now runs the Mermaid Inn with the help of her partner and co-owner, Jack Jameson. Her family has owned the Mermaid Inn since the early 1960s. Joanne's father, Joseph, was the previous owner. It hasn't functioned as an inn since they have owned it, though at one point her father did rent out three apartments upstairs until the family needed more space. Born and raised around a family of bar owners, Joanne has been working at the bar since the mid-1980s and owned it since 2010. With Joanne's guidance, the music has become the focus. Singer and songwriter Tom Gala started bringing the music to the bar. He encouraged Joanne to let him host open circle nights there once a month, a type of open mike night and gathering forum for musicians. From there it caught on. Word spread.

The Mermaid Inn does not pay the musicians, but the performers are allowed to charge a cover or pass a hat around at the bar. It functions as a performance space, a venue where they can play or sing in front of an audience.

To this day they don't advertise, except for a monthly calendar of events that's posted to their website. It's all word-of-mouth publicity; the musicians find them. That's the way it's been since the early 1980s, and it's remained that way ever since.

Bars like the Mermaid Inn are few and far between. That evening as the Old Time Jam session came to an end, the bar became eerily quiet. It wouldn't be that way for long. A short 24 hours later the bar would be filled with the fresh sounds of new singers and songwriters, anxious to showcase their music.

It's not often that you can hear styles like jazz, folk, blues, and rock music all in the same place. Where you can hear music that might have its roots its New Orleans, in small-town USA, in Ireland or England or Lithuania. Where you can shut your eyes and hear music that will transform you to a different era and time. This diverse atmosphere, along with the spirits at the inn—both alcohol and otherwise—should assure you a memorable night.

OLD ORIGINAL NICK'S ROAST BEEF

2149 S. 20TH ST. • PHILADELPHIA, PA 19145

(215) 463-4114 • NICKSROASTBEEF.COM

Magic of Meat and Gravy

The combo does not include fries. It doesn't even include a drink. The word *combo* only means that the meaty sandwich of your choice is topped with aged provolone cheese. Some might be disillusioned by this meaning of a combo. They might even feel a little disappointed at first. But their taste buds will prove otherwise once they bite into the juicy "combo" of tender meat, cheese, and homemade gravy that defines the Old Original Nick's Roast Beef sandwich.

Lili McKinney, co-owner and granddaughter of the original owners, Nick and Elsie DeSipio, takes pride in the quality of the food they serve day after day. She loves the food, confirms that she "could eat it every day." She often does.

She doesn't feel the same about the look of the place, maintaining that they keep the lighting darker and dimmer "because we don't want to show all the imperfections."

The imperfections are part of what makes this spot extraordinary, giving it an edge over every other beef-and-beer joint in this region of Philadelphia. Outside at this corner brick building on 20th and Jackson, there's a neon sign reading "Nick's Cafe" and a large window where you can see a few more neon beer signs hanging inside, but regardless of the time of day, it's usually too darkly lit to see what's going on inside. Dark but welcoming. The illuminating neon beer signs hanging all over the restaurant's interior are the main source of light. There's dated wood paneling covering the walls and plain tiled

139

floors, a long bar at the front of the restaurant, and simple dark wood tables in the back, with seating for approximately 75 people total.

The menu is even simpler, in the form of a few poster-board signs on the wall. Roast beef, roast beef combo, roast pork, roast pork combo, roast turkey, roast turkey combo. You get the idea. Simple, but full-of-flavor food that's served on small paper plates, barely large enough to accommodate the diameter of the sandwich.

When Nick's opened in 1938, there were three items: beef, pork, and ham. The signature dish today is still, discernibly, the roast beef sandwich. Layers of hand-sliced roast beef covered in gravy and served on a round Kaiser roll. The bottom of the roll is soggy, juicy, and moist. This meal is the kind of lick-your-fingers messy that's worth the messiness for a delicious meal.

The roast beef starts cooking at 11 p.m. every night to prepare for the next day's lunch service, an average fifty to eighty pounds of USDA prime beef round. It's slow cooked to perfection for about eight hours, then when lunch begins, it's displayed on the steam table, a small area set up at the far end of the bar, for the customers to drool over. If you come in for only a beer, there's a good chance that you'll stay for a sandwich once you notice that huge hunk of meat.

During the earlier years in business, Old Original Nick's Roast Beef, then known as just Nick's Roast Beef, was a regular hangout for men in uniform who worked at the Philadelphia Navy Yard. By the mid-1970s the neighborhood was changing, becoming a little less safe, and today it's changing again, this time, fortunately, becoming safer. Young people are moving into the neighborhood, and on the weekends Old Original Nick's is a great place to watch sports. You may even see some real live athletes on occasion. Eagles and Phillies players have been known to frequent the place.

The menu still includes the roast beef, pork, and ham. Today there's also turkey. There's even a vegetarian selection of broccoli rabe sandwiches, though if you're a vegetarian, I'm not sure why you'd choose to go to a place named Nick's Old Original Beef. Thanks to the addition of a self-contained fryer that Lili and Jeff added a couple of years ago, there are now fries.

If you're new to the city of Philadelphia, don't be confused by other Nick's Roast Beef establishments that you may see in the city. The family changed the name to Old Original after an unsuccessful business strategy in the 1960s. At one point there were around 13 locations, before they either closed or branched out on their own as entirely separate entities.

Today the family does own a few other newer locations. As of 1998, Jeff and Lili have been running a location in Springfield. More recently they also have an agreement with the Xfinity Live! Philadelphia center and a location in Westchester.

It's difficult to imagine when you talk to Lili that her career wasn't always in the family business. Her father, John, who owned it along with her mom, Ginette, from the early '60s until 1993, once told her, "You're going to get a real job first." She did. She was a teacher for 15 years before joining the family business. She hopes one day to retire, which seems a real possibility now that her children are taking an active role in the business. If you hang out there long enough, you'll feel like part of the family. Eddie, one of the managers, is already an honorary member. He's worked at Old Original Nick's since the early '80s. It's a real old-school joint.

P&F GIORDANO

1043 S. 9TH ST. • PHILADELPHIA, PA 19147

(215) 922-7819 • PANDFGIORDANO.COM

Not All Apples and Oranges

*T*here is one name you will never forget if you've lived in South Philadelphia for any period of time, especially if Washington Avenue happens to be one of your regular east–west cross streets. It's clearly spelled out on the corner of 9th and Washington, a huge sign in bold capitalized letters reading "Giordano." Below the sign, there's a myriad of fruit and produce exhibited on green makeshift tables, so much that you might think you are at an outdoor farmers' market in small-town America, not in the middle of a city of over 1.5 million people.

It's not an easy business to maintain, especially figuring out how to maintain it for about 100 years as the city and world change around you. Wally, one of the current co-owners of Giordano's, describes their strength as staying "flexible."

One example is the changing ethnic scene on South 9th Street— the Italian Market, a market that has becomes less Italian over the years, incorporating more Mexican and Asian influences, among other cultures. Some of the other long-standing Italian businesses seem distracted by this shift and get stilted by all of the changes.

P&F Giordano learns from the cultural shift. They hire new employees, work with them, and figure out how to adapt the types of products they buy and sell at their produce market to the tastes of the new ethnic groups who move into the neighborhood. Avocados were never as big a seller as they are today. Same for the persimmon.

They've managed to keep the original storefront that the first owners, Paul and Frances Giordano, purchased in 1921. Frances was the woman who helped bring it all together, a feisty Italian woman who worked out the deal herself. When one of the Giordano brothers died after serving in the US Army in the First World War, the family received a check from the government. Frances bought the building with that check.

Frances was well aware that to run a strong business, she would need help in the form of employees. Luckily she managed to provide that, too. She and Paul would have 14 children, all of whom would eventually be workers in the family business.

Just as the children multiplied, the money would eventually multiply, too. When the Great Depression swept through all of America, the Giordanos would manage to stay above it. By that point they had accumulated a large cash savings from working around the clock.

Exhaustion sets in when you work around the clock for an unforeseen period of time, so the Giordanos had a home remedy to prevent exhaustion: vinegar. It was splashed on their kids' faces regularly when they drove the trucks to the docks in New York to pick up produce. It kept them awake on their drive back to Philadelphia, often during the middle of the night, because they'd have to be back to the

store by the time it opened first thing in the morning and continue to work.

In later years, when the sons went off to war, this time for the Second World War, the six or seven daughters that remained at home would take over. Drive the trucks, carry on the business.

The owners of the P&F Giordano business today—John, Wally, and Eugene—never experienced any of this firsthand, but they heard the stories. They felt the burden of it, the sacrifices each and every one of the family members made to keep the business going. It's the reason why Wally still stands on the corner of 9th and Washington at least 12 hours daily, every day, working the cash register, helping customers, day in, day out, in rain, snow, sleet, or otherwise. To him, it's important to "keep moving forward." He also admits, jokingly, that he's a little fearful of all the ghosts in this place that would haunt him if he ever let this place go.

Over the years, the physical space of the building grew larger and larger. Every time an adjacent building became available, the Giordanos would buy it, turning the space into a warehouse that today extends almost the length of the entire street block. There's technically a massive "inside" space, but it's also open to the outside elements. Fruit and produce is the focus, but there are also products like fresh cheese and milk. A separate stand inside focuses on turkey wings and chicken wings by the pound, Cornish hens, and other kinds of smoked meat. Keep walking and you'll find large bags of dried pasta, tomato cans, and condiments like barbecue sauce and mustard.

Choose imported olive oil from a display rack that looks like it's been there since the store opened in 1921. The rack sinks in around the center, almost as a bed or a couch sinks in with age and use.

By midafternoon on the weekday I visited, the supply was dwindling. Empty cardboard boxes were piling up. The staff was cleaning up, getting ready to do it all over again the next day. There's something comforting about the consistency of it all. From an outsider's perspective, it appears the Giordano family also is content in the day-to-day intricacies of the business. Another day in business is a good one. Before they know it, they will be preparing for their centennial celebration.

Wally recalls a time when his aunt, almost 100 years of age herself at the time, stopped along the corner of 9th and Washington and rolled down the passenger window of the car. She had lived, worked, and breathed the Giordano produce business most of her life. At that point in her life she was too weak to get out of the car, but from inside she reached out, grabbed Wally's hand, and yelled out to him, "Just keep this place going."

PAT'S KING OF STEAKS

1237 E. PASSYUNK AVE. • PHILADELPHIA, PA 19147

(215) 468-1546 • PATSKINGOFSTEAKS.COM

A Cheesesteak Way of Life

No one ever said that running a business, especially a family business, was easy.

Then again, life wasn't quite so complicated in 1930 when hard-working brothers named Pat and Harry Olivieri spent their days running a hot dog stand. No one probably ever imagined that these two siblings selling hot dogs on the street would invent a new kind of food concoction called the Philly cheesesteak.

Or that this would then develop into a full-fledged, incredibly successful business that famous politicians, celebrities, and people from around the world would visit and wait patiently in long lines to get their taste of the iconic food that helped to make the city of Philadelphia famous.

Philly cheesesteaks are a way of life, and Pat's King of Steaks is credited as the inventor. It is the family's job to continue the legacy.

Over the years there have been quite a few family disagreements that have resulted in multiple legal battles over this family business, but I won't go into that here. What's important in the here and now is to show you the people behind Pat's today.

There's Frank Jr., who officially started working at Pat's when he was 11 years old. He began his career by cleaning counters because he was only allowed to work outside of the kitchen. Problem was, he was young and not yet tall enough to reach up to the counters, so he had to use an old metal milk jug as his stepping stool. As years passed he was given larger responsibilities, like working the soda window. Maybe even dropping in some fries.

Frank Jr. would probably be living somewhere in France by now had he made the decision to go to Le Cordon Bleu culinary arts school in Paris when he graduated from high school in 1982—that was his original plan. He always loved France and is quite possibly the only Italian American driving down South 9th Street in Philadelphia today who cranks out French bistro music from his car.

Instead, in 1982, his father needed help with the family cheese-steak business, so he agreed to stay "temporarily" in his hometown of Philadelphia to help him. Thirty-two years later, he's still there, beside his father, taking care of business every day.

Then there's Frank Jr.'s parents, Frank Sr. and his wife, Ritamarie, who have spent the majority of their lives on this triangular intersection where East Passyunk Avenue, South 9th Street, and Wharton Street meet. During the 45 minutes I spent outside the restaurant on a quiet weekday morning, I saw at least 10 people wave hello and

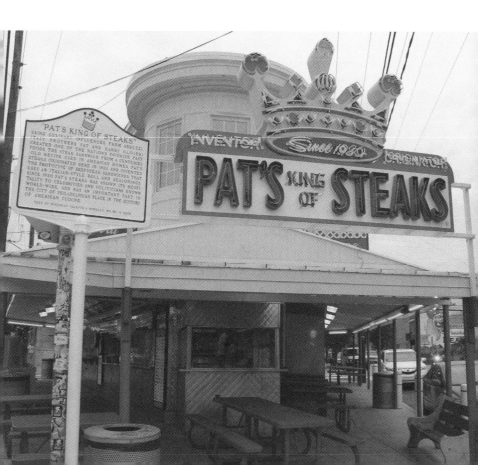

beep their horns as they saw Frank Jr., Frank Sr., and Ritamarie sitting outside together.

They spend so much time together that, like any family, they tend to talk over and around each other. When Frank Sr. showed up, Ritamarie gently told her husband to "go away" when he interrupted the interview for a casual chat. At another point of our conversation, Ritamarie told me about her fear of entering a certain country on her upcoming cruise vacation because of its recent link to a disease, while Frank Jr. glanced over in embarrassment at his mom's story. With only his eyes, he urged his mom to stop talking in the same way we all probably have done to our own parents over the years. Point is, it's all in fun, and it's amazing to watch the interaction live.

There are great, classic families that you might think only exist in the movies. I can tell you for a fact that families like this are real, and the Olivieris are the real thing.

The building where they sell the cheesesteaks hasn't changed too much over the years. When they opened, there were only stand-up counters bordering the building. Twenty-five years ago or so they decided it was time to add some customer seating, so they added picnic tables.

Over the years there were regular repainting projects to freshen up the building and make it feel newer. Around the year 2000, Frank Jr. decided to make a few changes to bring the building back and restore it to its original look. So, in a sense it went from old to newish to back to old again.

There are many of you who probably expect me to go into long details about the cheesesteak and how it's unique, but I won't do that here. Frank Jr. didn't really want to do it either. There's so much media attention and argument about who has the freshest cheesesteak ingredients, the most tender meat, the softest rolls . . . the list goes on and on.

You can decide for yourself, but, when it comes down to it, a cheesesteak is a few basic, key ingredients, including beef (thinly sliced, chopped, or "frizzled"), a long roll, melted cheese, and your choice of onions or other add-ons.

At Pat's, there are about 30 employees who work quickly to fulfill your cheesesteak craving. Tommy Francano might be one of them. He's worked at Pat's since the late '70s. Or maybe you'll see Sammy, who's been there since the early '80s. They know what they're doing. They can produce a sandwich at the window in six seconds or less. On an average busy weekend day, they easily sell a couple thousand sandwiches . . . per day! Cash only. Order cheesesteaks at one window. Go to the next window for fries and drinks. It's an assembly line of efficiency.

The only delay to that efficiency is the customer who's uneducated about the proper way to order a cheesesteak, and in today's world there might be more than a few customers like that. Many tourists regularly find their way to Pat's.

Frank Jr. said it best when he described it like this: "To understand Philadelphia is to understand cheesesteaks, and vice versa."

POP'S WATER ICE

1337 W. OREGON AVE. • PHILADELPHIA, PA 19148

(215) 551-7677 • POPSICE.COM

A Grand Slam Dessert

Filipo "Pop" Italiano was a smart man. He knew there was something missing in this area of South Philly. Thousands of Phillies baseball fans would regularly pass by Oregon Avenue, fans who would spend their days in the hot sun watching a four-hour-long baseball game, stuffing their mouths with salty snacks like soft pretzels, nachos, and fries. They might wash those snacks down with a cold beer, then by the end of the game, fans had two choices. They could easily forget about all the fun they just had by sitting in stadium traffic or by waiting in lines to get on overcrowded public transportation. Or they could continue the party with a fun, refreshing dessert at Pop's Water Ice. It was an easy decision to stop by Pop's.

Operations started off small, out of a street cart in South Philly, then expanded to a garage. Pop rented the garage from the people who lived in the building, until one day in the late 1950s when he bought it. He ran his entire business out of this 150-square-foot garage space until he retired. In the late 1980s the third-generation owners decided to renovate the space and turn it into what it is today: a glorified shed/warehouse industrial space triple the original size.

Even so, there are still no frills, and though there's more space for more water-ice machines and storage, the original character has remained.

No seats, no interior space for customers. Just a window that resembles the fast-food drive-thru window you see at a large, sprawling suburban shopping plaza. Except this one's in the middle of the fifth-most populous city in the US.

Without seats, you may wonder where you can sit down and relax. Look no farther than across the street, where there's a beautiful 19-acre park called Marconi Plaza, originally built to celebrate the 150th anniversary of the signing of the Declaration of Independence. When the plaza, modeled on Roman-style gardens, opened there's no doubt it was a hit with the large population of Italian Americans who lived nearby.

After all, Pop was one of them. The Pop's Water Ice website details the history of water ice. "It all began way back in ancient Rome when, on the hottest of days, the emperors sent the fastest runners high into the mountains to retrieve snow in pouches. The snow then would be mixed with seasonal fruits and honey." Today's water-ice-making process is a little more advanced. No one's running into the mountains to get snow.

Yet some processes have carried on exactly the same way as Pop started doing it over 80 years ago, like the lemons, which are hand squeezed in an old hand juicer. So fresh that you'll often bits of lemon and chunks of rind in your water ice.

Aside from the popular lemon flavor, customers now have a choice of about 15 additional flavors of water ice, ranging from mango to watermelon to the newest concoction for the fall months—pumpkin spice. Throughout the season they'll make 25 to 28 flavor varieties, and on a busy day around 400 quarts of water ice are consumed.

Then there's the gelato, the must-try for the ice cream fanatics (like me). A picture-perfect combo of water ice with ice cream, either hand dipped or soft-serve ice cream. Try the vanilla water ice with rocky-road ice cream combo. Delicious. And very cool.

What's even cooler, and I'm not talking about the water ice, is that Pop's is still there at its same physical location. At one point, Pop's tried their hand at the franchising business, but ultimately they stopped and returned their focus to their original location. (Note: There are still three other licensed stores that carry the Pop's Water Ice name, located in Sewell and Woodbury, New Jersey, and Havertown, Pennsylvania.)

The original location has original customers. Customers who went there as children can now bring their own children, grandchildren, or great-grandchildren.

There are special customers, too, of the nonhuman kind. Did you know that dogs love water ice? A number of people who visit Pop's purchase two water ices, one for themselves and one for their pet. One great story revolves around a police officer who showed up on horseback. He rewarded his ride for the day with a special treat of water ice.

Polly want a cracker? No, Polly actually wants a water ice. All the employees enjoy the regular customer who stops by with the talking parrot perched on his shoulder.

The six current owners of Pop's Water Ice are three sets of siblings who all worked their way through college by taking on a side job at Pop's. Not for the money but because it was just what you did. A family responsibility. One of the owners, Linda Raffa, remembers her parents saying, "It's a warm night. Better go help your granddad."

The owners all have other jobs that range from a special needs teacher to an accountant to an artist. Still, they all take turns in doing their part to continue running the Pop's Water Ice business, with the hope that it will one day pass to their own children, because as Linda says, it's important "just to keep the tradition going."

The operating season of Pop's Water Ice, usually around March 1 until mid-October, basically coincides with both the warmer weather and the Phillies season. They'll often extend their opening hours when the Phillies go into extra innings. To some residents of South Philly, opening day at the Phillies' stadium and opening day at Pop's is a special time of year. You know that winter is coming to an end.

RALPH'S ITALIAN RESTAURANT

760 S. 9TH ST. • PHILADELPHIA, PA 19147

(215) 627-6011 • RALPHSRESTAURANT.COM

✦

Thanks for the Memory

*A*mericans love Italian food. Forgive the typecasting, as I realize it might be a slight exaggeration to claim that every single American in the US loves Italian food, but there is definitely a large percentage of us. One that can probably be proved easily enough once you start counting and observing the Italian restaurants in your region, city, or state. The total number has to reach the hundreds of thousands, maybe millions. So when a South Philadelphia restaurant holds the title of the "oldest family-owned Italian restaurant" in the entire country, that's kind of a big deal.

Jimmy Rubino Jr., co-owner of Ralph's Italian Restaurant, is honored by the title, but it's not ultimately what motivates him. He's more focused on continuing to do what's been done every day for the last 115 years in business: Make quality food, create a memorable dining experience, and make the customers happy. Every day he feels "humbled that Ralph's Italian Restaurant has a loyal following."

Along with the loyal following of customers come equally loyal business relationships. One of those is with the local jeweler. That's because the restaurant is often the place where people want to celebrate their special occasions, whether that's a birthday, an anniversary, or an engagement. Recently there were four engagements at the restaurant over the course of a month.

Regardless of whether you come to Ralph's for a special occasion or an everyday occasion, you'll experience a friendly, intimate environment where customers are often known by name and greeted with hugs and kisses. It's all part of the overall experience while dining

on one of the three floors of this old boardinghouse from the late 1800s.

In 1900 Francesco and Catherine Dispigno opened up a restaurant on Montrose Street in South Philadelphia. By 1915 the business had grown, and the small restaurant on Montrose was too small for the amount of customers they gained, so they moved to the place where they're still located today at 760 S. 9th St.

If you're dining today on the third floor, a room outlined with an exposed brick wall and stained-glass windows embellished with grapes and wine bottles, you might feel the energy in the room, which was a home to Italian immigrants who migrated to the US in the 1920s, '30s, and '40s. At one point Jimmy's grandfather sponsored people to come over and gave them a place to live until they were established.

You might feel the same type of energy on the second floor, the interior of which is still about 80 percent original. Colorful painted murals on the wall capture various Italian scenes and are surrounded by dark, rich wood paneling, complemented by the wooden doors and windows at the front of the room.

The second floor once functioned as a changing space for staff to dress into their formal uniforms; red velvet vests were a signature part of that uniform. When Jimmy began helping out at the restaurant at 5 years of age, his mother, Elaine, spent days searching every store in Philadelphia to find a kid's red velvet vest that would resemble the staff's uniform. She finally found one at Strawbridge & Clothier. Jimmy would carry his uniform from their house next door to the second floor of the restaurant and change with the rest of the waitstaff.

The first floor was one that originally looked "dated," so in the early 1990s, they began the renovations. As they started jackhammering the floor, Jimmy noticed another floor underneath, the original tiled floor, most of which was still intact.

Today you'll see that original 1915 floor when you dine at Ralph's. When you do, remember the feeling that Elaine had when they surprised her with the renovations. She cried. A flood of memories from her childhood at the restaurant washed over her.

The simplest way to describe the type of food you'll find at Ralph's is "Italian classics with hearty portions," but they pride themselves on the unseen "spices," or passion they're putting into the cooking. Jimmy believes that "there'll be a difference in the way a dish tastes

Vintage Spots: Italian Restaurants

DANTE & LUIGI'S, CORONA DI FERRO: EST. 1899

Ralph's holds the title, but Dante & Luigi's claims to have been around longer. Though there are no records to verify the date, there are plenty of records to verify the amazing Old World Italian food served in beautiful old surroundings. Located in two converted townhouses from the 1850s, owners Michael and Connie LaRussa restored the interior to preserve its 19th-century features.

726 S. 10th St.; (215) 922-9501; danteandluigis.com

SALOON RESTAURANT: EST. 1967

Antique signs and a dark wood decor throughout make this place and its many rooms an intimate, classic Italian dining experience, as do the rumors and stories of the Italian Mafia who may dine there. There is frequent live music at the bar, and the place also has a great reputation for its wonderful and attentive service.

750 S. 7th St.; (215) 627-1811; saloonrestaurant.net

when a chef has love in his heart for what he does." When you enter the restaurant today, there's a good chance you'll see one of the family members, like Jimmy or his brother, Eddie, also a co-owner. You might see their mom, Elaine, who is still in charge of all the bookkeeping. You might see other staff members, many of the same ones who you would have seen if you dined at the restaurant 10 or 15 years ago.

When Jimmy's son Ryan, who's currently running a second Ralph's location in King of Prussia, told his father that he wanted to come back to the family business, Jimmy said that it was "one of the greatest moments of my life."

The family business carries on, with no prospect of coming to an end anytime soon. Eddie's daughter Alexis now has two young children, meaning a possible sixth generation. Ralph's Italian Restaurant in the 22nd century? Seems likely.

RAY'S HAPPY BIRTHDAY BAR

1200 E. PASSYUNK AVE. • PHILADELPHIA, PA 19147

(215) 365-1169 • THEHAPPYBIRTHDAYBAR.COM

Something to Laugh About

*L*ess than five minutes into our conversation and the interview had already swayed from serious to funny. "Two Italian guys living in South Philly are talking. One says to the other one, 'Me and my wife's 25th anniversary is coming up next week.' The other guy asks, 'What are you doing special for it?' First guy answers, 'I'm taking her to Italy.' Other guy exclaims, 'Wow that's great. What are you ever going to do on the 50th anniversary?' First guy answers, 'Pick her up.'"

Lou Capozzoli, owner of Ray's Happy Birthday Bar, will tell that same joke 10 times a day to customers who pass through his bar door. His bar is also his stage, and on that stage, his personality is colorful and vibrant enough to provide him his own long running one-man show.

In his past life, before he took over the bar that his father started in 1938, Lou was a musician touring around the country, entertaining, singing, and playing saxophone. Today, he is still a musician. He often plays his music and tells his jokes in front of a live crowd at the bar. The only difference is that he has a second job that takes up a whole lot of his time—a bar owner has a lot of responsibilities. It also means no more touring but, instead, taking advantage of his home base in South Philly.

On the wall, there's a framed collage of newspaper clippings and photos of South Philly musicians, including a big photo from one of those South Philly greats, often credited as Philly's first rock star, Charlie Gracie. Grab a beer and explore the bar's walls, where you'll

find various collages of famous musicians and old film stars. You might find great newspaper clippings and stories, too, some of Lou's band and articles about the bar, like when they celebrated their 75th bar anniversary in 2013. It's a museum without the entrance fee.

Speaking of entrances, the bar caters to those who feel like having a beer or a shot at almost any time, beginning at seven in the morning, every day of the week, except for Sunday (due to Pennsylvania alcohol laws). Over the years there have been some crowds who appreciate that early opening time, particularly weekend-shift workers from the local hospital who celebrate their Friday nights out on Monday mornings.

Some of those crowds might just show up at Ray's Happy Birthday Bar to celebrate their birthdays. If so, it's obviously a good place, not just because it's in the name of the bar, but because you get a free cake-flavored vodka shot on your actual birthday. The shot glass is inside a sleeve that holds a birthday candle, which is lit. You're given a big "Happy Birthday" hat to wear, and they take a picture for their website and Facebook page. If it's your birthday and you've already started the celebration, remember to take the glass out before you drink the shot so you don't burn your nose. Lou is always surprised by how many people he has to remind to do that.

All in all, it's an effective gimmick to get people to celebrate their birthday there, except for the rare few who visit for a free shot and then leave (don't do that!), but also it's significant to the bar's history. Lou's father, Anthony "Ray," used to welcome customers with "Happy Birthday" instead of hello. After Anthony passed away, Lou changed the name of the bar from Ray's Bar to Ray's Happy Birthday Bar to honor his father's memory.

Anthony bought the bar in 1938 when it was called La Rosa Cafe. When Lou was born in 1939, his family moved above the bar, and he was raised here. Then the war broke out. In 1943, while his father was in the army, his mother ran the bar. They were poor and struggling, but Lou still has great memories of running downstairs to the bar to get cornflakes and milk while his mother worked. As time passed, they eventually remodeled in the early 1950s. For a time the bar also functioned as a seafood restaurant and even a sports bar. Lou reminisces about how loud it used to be upstairs when a fight was on the TV downstairs. Lots of cheering and yelling until there was one break of silence when the winner was announced.

Inside Ray's today the clientele is a mixture of locals and tourists—many of whom come in after getting their Philly cheesesteak around the corner at Pat's or Geno's. Except for the new kind of crowd, it still probably feels the same as it did when Anthony owned the place, partly because it's one of the few bars in Philly where you're still allowed to light up a cigarette. Many of the interior features have not changed since the 1950s. The bar's the same, the water trough where the men used to spit their tobacco under the bar is still there, the mirrors in the back room are even still there, along with a separate entrance that was at one point considered the "ladies' entrance." Lou has added some of his own personal touches to enhance the overall feel and character of the place. What was once an ugly old, bland air-conditioning duct in the back room is now transformed into a mural with a picture of a musician and the phrase "Music Makes Me Smile."

The personal touches give the place an inviting atmosphere that you don't see at lots of bars. Knowing Lou's story and all the special memories that are a part of this place, it's not surprising that this place is like Lou's home. You'll be welcomed here as if it were your home, too, regardless of whether your home is a half mile away or 5,000 miles away. Just come prepared to laugh.

SARCONE'S BAKERY

758 S. 9TH ST. • PHILADELPHIA, PA 19147

(215) 922-0445 • SARCONESBAKERY.COM

+≒≒+

Seedy and Sensational

Some discover this place via a guide when they disembark from a big Philly tour bus and stroll through the Italian Market. This is one of the featured spots.

Some discover it via a nerdy-looking two-wheeled vehicle—a Segway—that glides through the city streets. Wearing helmets and gliding through the Italian Market in a pack, these customers are always easy to spot.

Others don't need to discover it. It's a place they've been going regularly for as long as they can remember. It's where their parents, grandparents, and probably even great-grandparents got their bread.

Inside Sarcone's Bakery, it's not a normal nine-to-five lifestyle. Some begin work at midnight, others at 2 a.m. and a few others at 4 a.m. The pizza makers come in around 7 a.m. While you sleep, the real magic is happening. The mixers are in full force. The brick oven is reaching its peak temperature. The smell of fresh bread is filling up the bakery and wafting out into the street. It's almost enough to make you want to jump out of bed early.

The real magic has to happen during these hours in order to supply an average of 1,500 loaves of bread a day to Sarcone's customers, including retail customers and wholesale customers like restaurants throughout the city. That's just a normal weekday. It might double to 3,000 loaves on a Saturday.

It's shocking to hear those numbers when you see the building where it all happens. The original building is the retail shop that you see today. That building once functioned as both the bakery and the shop. The brick oven was once in the basement of the same building. The look of the retail shop today hasn't changed much since 1918. There are a few wooden display cases filled with products like tomato pies, Italian breadsticks, biscotti, and cookies. There are baskets behind the counter, filled with all their bread varieties that come in a number of sizes. There's space for about five customers to fit comfortably inside. It's small, but it serves the purpose. Come prepared to order by having enough cash. This place is cash only.

The shop expanded in the 1930s when the Sarcones acquired a flower shop next door and transformed the building into a bakery. Today there are four brick ovens and a couple of industrial-size dough mixing machines in a second adjoining building. The machines help to ensure consistency with a check-and-balance system.

There is also a human check-and-balance system. Usually that's in the form of Louis, who comes in every morning prepared for a serious inspection. He questions his staff, but, more importantly, he questions his son Lou, who takes the brunt of it: "Why is it like this? Why is it like that?" Another way to achieve consistency.

Inside the store on the bakery's walls, you'll notice some pictures of the previous generations who have run the business. This is the

foundation of Sarcone's Bakery, five generations of family members who have carried on the tradition of baking bread. Today that business is run by Louis Sarcone Jr. ("Louis") and Louis Sarcone III ("Lou"). Sarcone's bread is a great foundation to many of the best Philly cheesesteak and hoagie sandwich shops throughout the city. To service their wholesale clients, Sarcone's make regular-size steak rolls (7 to 8 inches in length), small steak rolls, and small Kaiser rolls.

But the traditional Italian bread loaf is enough to satisfy anyone's bread craving. It is long, measuring 18 to 20 inches, and topped with sesame seeds. The seeded bread is what has made Sarcone's famous. It takes six hours to make, and the Sarcones are proud to confirm that they don't take shortcuts, as some bakeries often do, in order to decrease the time it takes to make the bread.

When Luigi Sarcone started Sarcone's Bakery in 1918, he believed in keeping things the same. No machines. All handmade in the exact sense of the word. It wasn't until around 50 years after opening that they began using a few machines to improve efficiency. It's difficult to produce 1,500 loaves of bread a day when you're making it all by hand.

Transitioning to machines was a major change and a win for the younger generation back in the late '60s. A machine was purchased, but due to the older generation's strict philosophy of "no change," it was not actually used until almost 10 years later.

Today Louis has that same no-change philosophy when it comes to their everyday operational processes. In the age of computers, the Sarcones have figured out a way to keep things "vintage." Their current system functions as it always has, using no more than a well-documented book, a phone and voicemail system, and handwritten receipts. Lou hopes to change that. One day. Like the transition to machines to help produce the bread, it will be the same type of slow transition from paper to computers. Hopefully this transition won't be 10 years, though.

What you can count on is that the younger generations will always test the older generations. That's how it worked throughout their history.

They won't mess with certain things, though, the most important one being the bread recipe, the same one that's been used for almost 100 years, and the main source to bake the bread—the old-school brick ovens built into the walls.

SHANE CONFECTIONARY

110 MARKET ST. • PHILADELPHIA, PA 19106

(215) 922-1048 • SHANECANDIES.COM

Molds of Joy

$\mathcal{J}$t was almost a tragedy. Fortunately, they heard what happened before it was too late. Ryan called Eric with the news, and soon after they met behind the church, where they retrieved the old antique piano next to the dumpster and pushed it down the streets of Old City to its new home at the Franklin Fountain. They saved it from destruction.

In much the same way, brothers Ryan and Eric Berley saved the Shane Confectionary business when they decided to purchase it in 2010. They're passionate about preserving antiques, whether that be an old antique piano or a historic candy business that in its own right is a kind of antique. Restoration projects were few and far between during the previous 30 years of Shane Confectionary's life. The building was "falling into the sidewalk, literally," Ryan told me. Yet the confectionary store was an important part of Philadelphia's past, and the fact that its home was in Old City, a short half mile away from the Liberty Bell and the place where the Declaration of Independence was signed, was also rather important.

They embarked on an 18-month renovation to restore it back to its original allure. Saved and restored the once stunning curved glass windows, added antique tiles to the foyer where there had previously been poured concrete, even removed asbestos tile and repaired the entire fire escape.

They wouldn't have done all this had it not been for the gems preserved inside the store. Hundred-year-old antique cash registers and ornately designed casework, original copper kettles used to cook the cream, and old scales for measuring out the weight of the confections.

To preserve its history as a candy store from the past, Ryan and Eric brought their own antiquing expertise into each and every detail. When another old candy store in the Philadelphia area was closing, they were able to salvage the Pennsylvania German hard-candy molds, then use those molds to create striking clear candy toys to display and sell in the shop. They've collected over 1,000 molds now.

Regardless of your age, you're guaranteed to find something exciting at Shane Confectionary. Buttercreams, fudge, chocolate-covered pretzels, brandied cherries, licorice, and rock creams. Nostalgic candy like Necco Wafers, Bonomo Banana Turkish Taffy, and Abba-Zabas. For those who want to take home a piece of Philadelphia, try the Liberty Bell pops. For the adventurous types, try the dark-chocolate-covered bacon, cooked in-house and hand-dipped in dark chocolate.

The in-house cooking happens throughout the three floors of the 110 Market St. building. Ice-cream making takes place on the first floor, the candy kitchen is on the second floor and the chocolate-dipped production is on the third floor. Ryan and Eric also own the

Franklin Fountain, an ice-cream parlor and soda-fountain business a few buildings down at 116 Market St. Though this parlor is only technically 10 years old, it, too, looks like a scene from an old black-and-white movie. Both Shane Confectionary and the Franklin Fountain are the epitome of the word *vintage.*

Considering the Berleys' own past, it's fitting.

They literally grew up in an antiques shop. The front room of their home was devoted to their parents' shop. Through the years it turned into a lifestyle. Taking the boys on the road to antiques shows on the weekends. Then buying trips, at least two weeks every summer, where they would travel together in an empty van across small town America, and come back with a van packed full of newly purchased old antiques.

Both Ryan and Eric embraced all these experiences and memories. They embarked on their own adventures to learn more about ice-cream and candy stores prior to becoming business owners. They traveled across Europe and the US, visiting every old ice-cream shop and candy store they could discover. Prior to starting the Franklin Fountain, Ryan worked at Freeman's, America's oldest auction house, located on Chestnut Street in Philadelphia.

It's spectacular to see how the Berleys carried that over into an old historic candy-making shop. Considering recent findings on its past uses, it's miraculous that the building has survived more than 150 years.

William Herring and Daniel Dengler first used this building as a working confectionary business beginning in 1863. Since the candy business is typically more of a winter business, they needed to find a side plan to keep things going in the summer. Turns out that Daniel Dengler's other specialty was fireworks, so seemingly during the 1870s and '80s there were both a fireworks shop and a confectionary shop operating at 110 Market St. Anyone who knows a thing or two about fires probably realizes that housing fireworks at the same place that you also use gas kettles could be a real catastrophe.

Luckily, no explosions occurred, and William Wescott purchased the confectionary shop in 1899 and ran it until 1910. The next era of the operation was an important one, when, at the age of 31, Edward Shane purchased the candy store. A well-respected man, he turned the confectionary shop into a destination. Over the years, people would come in to get a taste of his homemade buttercreams and marshmallows or various recipes of homemade chocolate bliss. The Shane family kept the tradition going for almost another 100 years.

The Berleys will now continue that tradition. There's no doubting their passion. Eric even made time for the candy business during his honeymoon, when he and his wife took a trip to visit the world's oldest candy store in Paris, France.

It's more than just a candy business.

SMOKEY JOE'S

210 S. 40TH ST. • PHILADELPHIA PA 19104

(215) 222-0770 • SMOKEYJOESBAR.COM

Characters on the Walls

C ustomers experience a range of emotions when they see the bar's wall decorations. Some laugh, some smile, some squirm, and a few turn red in embarrassment.

That's because the walls are filled with hundreds of framed pictures. New pictures, old pictures, and older pictures. Pictures of previous decades of University of Pennsylvania ("Penn") football players and students, and customers of Smokey Joe's bar.

Recently a Penn student came in and searched the walls, only to break out in tears of laughter when he finally found what he was looking for—a picture of his father during his days at Penn. "That's when I know I'm getting old," says Paul Ryan Jr., co-owner of Smokey Joe's, who has a clear recollection of when that customer's father was a regular customer at Smokey Joe's Bar.

Smokey Joe's was officially established in 1933, the 96th license given out in the state of Pennsylvania after Prohibition ended; it was originally located at 36th and Walnut Streets. In 1952, Paul's father, Paul Ryan Sr., purchased the bar. Paul Ryan Sr. grew up in the bar business and learned about the business from his father, who owned a number of neighborhood bars. His father thought he was crazy to buy a college bar because he didn't think college kids could drink. Boy, was he wrong!

Paul Sr. was well respected and well known throughout the Penn community. During his tenure as owner, Smokey Joe's became renowned as the "Pennstitution," particularly after it earned acknowledgment from Gerald Ford, who, during his commencement address

in 1975, joked that Smokey Joe's Bar was the "17th institution of higher learning," after the other 16 Penn learning facilities at the time.

Over the years that the Ryan family has owned Smokey Joe's, the bar has moved several times—to 38th Street in 1961 then to 40th Street in 1978—a result of redevelopment efforts as the Penn campus grew and changed.

Regardless of the location, its popularity, its character, and its reputation have remained consistent. More importantly, its presence has become a fixture as part of the college campus and as Philly's University City neighborhood bar. You know it'll always be somewhere on and around the campus even if its physical location sometimes changes.

Today the interior, denoted in colors of mustard yellow, browns, and deep reds, is classic old-American beer bar. The long wraparound bar occupies close to one-half of the place. Tables and booths covered by red-and-white checkered tablecloths take up the other half. Next to the booths there's graffiti sketched with the names of the college students who have frequented Smokey Joe's in past years.

It's a typical bar with all the normal beer and shot selections, but on Tuesday through Sunday you can also order food. Smokey Joe's has partnered with Enjay's Pizza (enjayspizza.com) to serve the

Vintage Spots: Cigar Shops

HARRY'S SMOKE SHOP: EST. 1938

Always one of the only places in Old City to get a cigar, this place has changed locations and owners over the years, but the most important thing has remained: It's been continuously selling cigars to the community since its established date of 1938. Cozy leather couches and chairs offer you a relaxed area in the back where you can enjoy it.

14 N. 3rd St.; (215) 925-4770; harryssmokeshop.com

TWIN SMOKE SHOPPE: EST. 1950

What was once a candy shop, a Hallmark card store, and a place to buy cigars turned into a cigar-only establishment when customers "complained about the cards smelling like cigars," owner Anthony Renzulli informed me. Check out the amazing original stone foundations when you head to the back of the store and enter the "Rocky Patel Lounge." And don't miss Anthony's personal vintage collection of games and toys, including Mr. Potato Head and the Beatles Yellow Submarine figurine, in a glass display case when you enter the store.

1537 S. 10th St.; (215) 334-0970; twinsmokeshoppe.com

perfect food to soak up the beer, which includes pizza, hoagies, and a few great bar starters like fries, garlic knots, and chicken wings.

If you are sitting at one of those tables or booths, you will have a nice view of the small stage at the back of the room, where on a Sunday night you will usually hear live music from fellow Penn students. On Tuesday that stage becomes the spotlight for Kenn Kweder, a musician and native of southwest Philly, who has been a memorable part of the Philadelphia music scene since the late 1960s. On weekends DJs regularly set up shop so the bar also turns into a dancing venue.

If you prefer a quieter scene, then stop by for a drink after a hard day of classes and unwind in the late afternoon, like the day I visited, when there was a small group of about 10 customers around the bar and the song "Lean On Me" played from the speaker.

If you just want the best place in the vicinity to drink cheaply, then consider stopping by during the Monday all-day happy hour or Wednesday during what they called a "sink or swim" night. You pay a cover and then get 50-cent drinks the rest of the night.

Regardless of the atmosphere, it's always been the signature Penn college bar, a bar steeped in tradition, much like the university.

On the way out as you leave the bar, you'll walk past a wall of painted caricatures and a framed poster filled with pictures and labeled "Hall of Fame Inductees." That's the Smokey Joe's personal hall of fame, a spoof on some of the regular customers, a first indication of the characters and the stories that have passed through these doors.

Come in during homecoming or alumni weekends at the school, where the packed-in crowds become even more packed in, and where you're guaranteed to meet some of these characters and hear some of the fun stories firsthand.

Stories that all took place at this one bar. A bar that's created thousands of great memories at college for decades worth of customers.

As Paul Ryan Jr. describes it, it's a "neighborhood bar where the neighborhood is made up with people from all over the world. And the neighborhood changes every four years." Can't get much better than that.

SNOCKEY'S OYSTER AND CRAB HOUSE

1020 S. 2ND ST. • PHILADELPHIA PA 19147

(215) 339-9578 • SNOCKEYS.COM

Keep Shucking On

Smart business owners understand that you need loyal customers for your business to have continued longevity. If you want to have a contest for the "most loyal customer" award, measured by the greatest number of years that person's been a customer, Snockey's Oyster and Crab House would win by a landslide. That customer is 99 years old and has been coming to Snockey's since her grandparents first brought her there when she was 8. Ninety-one years!

It's stories like this that help keep the current owners of Snockey's, brothers Ken and Skip Snock, "shucking on" every day, that stop them from calling it quits, that keep them committed to a business that has a very unequal balance of work to life.

The man who started this business was Ken and Skip's grandfather Frank, who opened his first Oyster house at 142 South St. in Philadelphia in May 1912. That was a busy year for Frank. He was 21 years old and only had about $50 to his name, enough to set up a business. To pay for the rent, a $4 mercantile license, purchase a keg of beer and some oysters. Around that same time, his wife, Rose, gave birth to their first child on the second floor of that oyster house. Two days after giving birth she went back to work at the oyster house. She worked there for 79 more years. For Rose's entire life she lived on top of the restaurant.

Two of the couple's four children, Ed and Bob, became the second generation to work in the business. In the 1930s, Frank opened a

Vintage Spot: Seafood

anastasi seafood: est. 1908

You can sit down at simple tables in the middle of this fish market with a full service bar and get your choice of fresh fish and seafood from a fourth-generation Italian family, whose grandfather started out selling fish from a cart that he pushed through the streets.

1101 S. 9th St.; (215) 462-0550; anastasiseafood.com

second restaurant in Atlantic City during the summer months, and Ed worked in the restaurant. Ed's life changed in 1938 when they posted a sign in the window—"Waitress Wanted"—and a young girl from New Orleans showed up for a job. That woman became Ed's wife, and they were married before he went off to war for 5 years. After the war, Ed and Bob ran the restaurant for another 50 years or so. It survived through rough times, when four children slept in the same bed during the winter to keep warm because the heat never made it to the third floor. It survived through two World Wars. It survived through the Depression.

The third generation officially took over in the '90s, though they've also lived and breathed the business. Ken and Skip Snock have been working at Snockey's since they were kids. I asked Skip if he's always liked the oyster and seafood business. He looks me straight in the eye to say, "I never liked it. I'm still not thrilled with it," and then he smiles. It's hard work, and choosing to take ownership in the business came with a lot of sacrifices, but both he and Ken don't seem to have any inclination to call it quits yet.

I asked Ken what's changed in the last 100 or so years. That's a complex question. In some ways, not much has changed.

There's still that same traditional interior, and though they've had to move locations a few times, it's still modeled after the design of the original location. I confess I don't know much about the way oyster houses should look, so Ken described it to me like this: "An oyster house should be white tiles, white walls, minimalistic. It shouldn't try to be fancy." They moved to their newest location in 1975. They took a few things with them as they moved, like the back bar (originally built in 1932) that you see inside the restaurant today. There used to be a stand-up bar counter only. Now there are a few barstools. If you look at the framed picture of one of the original Snockey's locations, you'd have no idea it was a different place. They modeled it after the original. A front bar with a few cocktail tables and a back restaurant section with modest tables and chairs.

A traditional interior should be equally paired with traditional food.

There are still oysters, crab, clams, and steaks, just like there was in 1912.

It's evolved a bit. Today there's a lot more broiled than fried options, due to the health-conscious environment we live in now. There's more variety than there was before. Today you have your choice of up to a dozen oyster varieties and three different types of clams on the raw bar. You can choose to have your lobster whole or stuffed with crabmeat, your steak a porterhouse or filet mignon. You can get your shrimp fried, stuffed, Cajun, or popcorn style. Your fish choices range from flounder to bluefish or maybe even salmon.

In practice, though, it's all a very traditional seafood selection, and that's the way they want to keep it. Ken said he "doesn't read fancy French cookbooks."

There's still the same tried-and-true oyster stew recipe, their grandmother's original recipe, and Ken believes that "lightning would come hit me in the head if we ever made it another way," a sure sign from his grandmother's spirit watching down on them.

To honor those previous generations, it's important not to take any shortcuts that might compromise the quality of your products. Ken describes it best: "If you want to stay in business 102 years, you can't take the shortcuts." True. Very true.

STOCK'S BAKERY

2614 E. LEHIGH AVE. • PHILADELPHIA, PA 19125

(215) 634-7344

✢

Pleasure by the Pounds

It's a fitting name—pound cake—because you can measure its weight in pounds. Most weigh a couple pounds each. Heavy enough that if you carried it around for an entire day, you may even build some muscle strength in your arms. Compare the pound cake to weight classes at a wrestling match and it would be in the heavyweight category for cakes. All of these depictions define the pound cake, and in Philadelphia, there's one bakery that's pinned down all of its competitors since the mid-1920s, Stock's Bakery in North Philadelphia.

The pound cake sounds basic enough, made from a few even more basic ingredients like flour, eggs, butter, and sugar. Knowing this, it may appear simple to bake the perfect pound cake just by following the recipe.

Until, that is, you understand at Stock's Bakery, there is no recipe. Mark Stock, co-owner, explains, "We don't deal with recipes; we deal with formulas."

His grandfather Frank Stock created the formula back in the mid-1920s that they're still mixing together today. Frank may not have chosen the baking profession had it not been for his father, Mark's great-grandfather Joseph Stock, who emigrated from Germany to Philadelphia. From 1919 on, Joseph ran a bread bakery.

Frank wanted to bake, but he wanted to branch out from only bread baking, so he attended an institute in New York and studied the science and chemistry of baking. Soon after Stock's famous pound cake formula was created. Today, three fourth-generation co-owners—Mark, Kristine, and Frank—are using those secret formulas to

catalyze the quantity of pound cakes they distribute to their customers and wholesalers.

On a visit to Stock's, in addition to pound cakes, you can choose from doughnuts, cinnamon buns, birthday cakes, butter cakes, pies, and Danishes, all delicious pleasures in their own right. But "pound cake is king," as Kristine affirms, meaning when there are pound cake orders to fill, Stock's will fill the oven with pound cakes and pound cakes only. If that means they have to make less of other products or eliminate other products altogether during a busy holiday season, they will. Pound cakes are the reason why, during those busy holiday seasons, customers stand in lines around the block.

Kristine labels her grandfather Frank as a "magician," because he understood how to fix any baking problem. If the dough was flat, Frank knew how to make it rise again. If there was no brown sugar, he could easily demonstrate how to make it from granulated sugar. Both Mark and Kristine credit their grandfather with teaching the family how to cook.

He also seemingly taught them the value of a strong work ethic. Mark began working at around 9 years of age. When the bakery was short of help, he would get a wake-up call at four in the morning. He'd work for two hours at the bakery before school even started. Their work schedules haven't changed much since they were kids.

Mark, Kristine, and Frank are regularly working seven days a week now. Their only respite is during the month of July, when they close the store to regain momentum for the next new season.

They're all getting regular family time together, only because most of the family is now working at the bakery. The fifth generation is working there today. Apart from the Stock family, there have been generations of other families who have worked and stayed at the store over the years, making it one big extended family.

As new generations get involved, the building has evolved. Karl Stock, the third generation, worked at the store from a young age before he eventually took over for his father, Frank, and for him the bakery wasn't just a place to work, but it was also his home, as he lived above the store in the same building. Though today Karl is retired, he still plays the role of "chief cook," making breakfast, lunch, and dinner for the staff as they work around the clock during the busy holiday seasons.

No one lives there anymore, but people still sleep there on occasion. It functions as a kind of dorm room, where employees can take naps on bunk beds during busy times.

Inside today, the store has a 1960s feel—the bakery display cases and the overall interior design of the store haven't changed much since the 1960s.

Inside you will believe you're in a past era, but outside the Stock family has had to deal with the reality that the world has changed. Recently the laws of the 21st century almost ruined their business: The city of Philadelphia implemented a ban on trans fats that affected all businesses, including small family-run bakeries like Stock's. This would have caused them to alter their famous pound cake formula, which in turn would have altered the famous taste. The Stock family put out a petition at the store. Customers took blank pages from that petition, passed them around to their friends and neighbors and to local companies, and then faxed and e-mailed them back to the Stock family. A woman raised her hand at the city council hearing, arguing, "I didn't invite you into my kitchen. Who are you to tell me what to eat? I'm 84 years old. I didn't need you before. I don't need you now." The city of Philadelphia gave in, and Stock's was exempted from the ban, giving them the freedom once again to make their pound cake the same way as they have been making it for the last 90+ years. Justice is restored.

SUPERIOR PASTA COMPANY

905 CHRISTIAN ST. • PHILADELPHIA, PA 19147

(215) 627-3306 • SUPERIORPASTA.COM

Impress Your Guests

Serving a gourmet Italian pasta feast for your spouse or loved one does not have to involve a day of laboring away in your kitchen. But that's not to say it won't involve a day of laboring in someone else's kitchen. Superior Pasta Company is ready for the laboring, and they also have the help of massive, industrial-size antique equipment that's been effectively mixing, sheeting, and rolling out homemade pasta since 1948.

The kitchen where it all happens is inside a private residential house transformed into a pasta company. "Manufacturing in a South Philly row home has its challenges," explains Joe, who joined the company after finishing college in 1999, the year his father, also named Joe, purchased Superior Pasta from the original family. Ever since then, the father-and-son duo has been running the show.

One of the challenges is the size of the kitchen itself. *Tiny* is the best word to describe it, barely the size of a walk-in closet, which means that usually only one or two people can be in the kitchen at any given moment. Fortunately, though, the rest of the floor space is spacious enough to fit the important stuff like the antique ravioli machine, pasta sheeter, and mixer. Because it's so antique, it can also be a little challenging when a part needs to be replaced or fixed on the machine. Luckily, they've managed to find solutions so far.

Carrying over the traditions that made Superior Pasta superior in the first place was important when Joe purchased the business. Joe remembers the great people who helped create those traditions, including people like Antoinette Ciccotelli, who was a regular

presence at Superior Pasta for most of her life, until she passed away in 1995. She would make the ravioli by hand with giant wooden rolling pins. Antoinette's neighbor Clara still worked at the store when Joe assumed ownership. She worked at the store for over 40 years and just passed away a few years ago at the age of 88. Documenting all those great recipes was an initial business challenge for Joe and Joe, considering there had been no recipe book previously, but then again Clara could not understand why anyone would ever need such a thing as a recipe book. She always had a book full of recipes in her head.

Today, that recipe book is filled with over 60 different products. Choose from 15 different kinds of ravioli packaged by the dozen. Some are focused on the cheese. There's three cheese, whole wheat cheese, and goat cheese flavors. Some are focused on the vegetables, like porcini mushroom or broccoli rabe. Some are specialty seafood flavors like crab, lobster, and shrimp. Then there are the classics like manicotti and lasagna. Seven different kinds of fresh-cut pasta, with choices including fettuccine, linguine, spaghetti, and capellini, pair wonderfully with over 10 different kinds of homemade gravy choices.

Too many choices? Then keep it simple and get one of the bundled dinner packages for two or four people, like the popular Nicolo's Eggplant Parmigiana (named after the original owner), which includes olive salad and sweet peppers stuffed with cheese and prosciutto, followed by eggplant parmigiana, a side dish of linguine with marinara sauce, freshly grated cheese, a loaf of homemade bread, and imported ice fruit sorbets for dessert.

Entrees are frozen directly after production and are very easy to prepare at home in the microwave or oven. A pamphlet with cooking instructions is provided, making it easy for you to have a gourmet dinner at home, whether or not you know anything about cooking at all. The only thing you need to know is how to turn on the oven or push the Start button on the microwave.

The benefits of having a pasta business in South Philly, around the corner from South 9th Street and in the Italian Market neighborhood, is that you have easy access to any products you need to put inside your pasta. That might be fruit and produce from the shop next door or fresh meat at the butcher's shop a block up the street.

Step inside to the simple, old-school store, and, at first impression, it looks like a small convenience store. One wall is filled with products that you might pair with your Italian meals, like olive oil, dried pasta, olives, and spices. Next is a wall of floor-to-ceiling refrigerators and freezers. Unlike a convenience store where the refrigerators are filled with water and sodas, these refrigerators hold the good stuff—all that homemade pasta.

At the back of the store is another small display case and a counter, where you'll usually be greeted by the older of the two Joes. Born and raised in this area, his parents brought him to this store often when he was a child. He became a regular customer and was well acquainted with the previous staff and owners, so when the chance came along to purchase the store, he knew it was one opportunity he didn't want to miss.

The younger Joe and the older Joe seem to balance each other. While the older Joe communicates and chats with the in-person customers, the younger Joe assists in communicating with the online customers. That involves sites like Facebook, their online ordering through their own website, and recently a relationship with Amazon-Fresh. They ship their products nationally. All this means you should not consider looking at the frozen-dinner display in your supermarket ever again, especially if you're in the South Philly vicinity.

So invite your date over for a romantic dinner, or impress your spouse with a special meal at home. All you have to do to prepare is push a button on the microwave or oven.

SWIACKI MEATS

3623 SALMON ST. • PHILADELPHIA, PA 19134

(215) 634-0820 • SWIACKIMEATS.COM

Long Live the Kielbasa

𝓝 ot only does kielbasa have a fun name, but it's also a delicious, wonderful food creation, particularly for those of us who are sausage lovers. Still, I didn't really believe her story at first. "Eating kielbasas keeps you alive," Cathy rationalized, as she shared the story of her father-in-law, Ed, one of the original owners and founders of Swiacki Meats. He was 98 years old when he passed away.

It's not a proven fact. Yet, the day I visited, there was some indescribable feeling in the Swiacki Meats building, where Ed Swiacki, the elder Ed's son, was working along with his wife, Cathy; their son, Eddie; and other family members like Wes and Ray. It was almost like a burst of energy, quite possibly coming from the amazing family dynamic in the room. They argue and joke about past times. One cousin remembers, "You let him off work to play baseball, but you would never let me off."

During the busiest times they bring on more family members to help them keep up with demand. Christmas and Easter holidays for the Swiacki family members are filled with togetherness, but that togetherness doesn't come in the form of relaxation. It's all work. Even the grandchildren are now regular helpers during the holiday operation, participating in work like stocking the shelves and sharpening pencils.

If you're a new customer, you will be noticed, mostly because there is a large population of old customers. Not always old in age, more so "old" in the sense that they have been coming to Swiacki

Meats since they were children. For many loyal customers, it wouldn't be Christmas or Easter holiday season without first standing in line to get your kielbasas. Those lines frequently extend around the block, and it may take an hour and a half until you get to place your order. Good news is while you're waiting in that line, you'll often get some free kielbasa samples.

Most of the family who's still working here today has been working together for quite a few years, too. Around 40 years. Maybe a little more, though Cathy wouldn't give me an exact number because she's worried she is getting old, in the real sense of the word. She's not. Her passion for the Swiacki Meats business, the same as it was 40-some years ago when she first started, reminds me of a young, bright-eyed girl who's just found out she got her dream job.

On the other hand, there are some old things about this store, and Cathy usually greets new customers by saying, "Welcome to the '50s." True. This shop is as authentic as it gets. No-frills in the entire sense of the word. White walls; long, plain display cases; and wire shelving. A few signs and pictures on the walls. A chalkboard with the description of the meats and cheeses they have available for sale. A framed newspaper article from 20 years ago, when they received a beautiful review and were titled the "Kielbasa Kings."

Near the entrance in one of the tall refrigerators you'll see plastic bags filled with 12 different varieties of homemade pierogis, labeled on the front of the refrigerator with handwritten pink sticky-note paper.

The store has a phone and a phone number you can call, but there's no mention of the phrase *online ordering* in the Swiacki Meats business. All orders are filled the old-fashioned way. In person. You have to visit the store. You have to actually talk to someone.

Staying consistent with the rest of the store's theme, there's the antique machinery and equipment in the back of the store, also mostly from the 1950s. These machines fulfill the most important functions in preparing the kielbasa, massive, old machines that grind and combine all the ingredients in a kielbasa, like the pork butt and right mix of spices, to create their own secret blend. There are ancient hand-built smokehouses and smoke racks. All of this is inside an unassuming building with red doors and a simple "Swiacki Meats" sign outside. They have to keep repainting the doors every so often, and it always has to be the color red, because as Cathy says, "Everyone knows we're behind the red doors."

Nothing else is really needed. Their products sell themselves.

They've made a few adjustments to their product line as customers' preferences and patterns of behavior change over the years. They used to sell many more roasts, which required a longer time in the oven and a full day of cooking. Today, more customers seem to take the "heat and eat" approach.

Cathy and Ed's son, Eddie, is now taking on a bigger role in the business. He's doing everything to continue the tradition his grandfather started, but he's also resourcefully added a few new products. Products like stuffed cabbage, smoked hot sausage with Colby Jack cheddar cheese and peppers, and new pierogi flavors like sweet potato, cheesesteak, and farmer cheese.

Cathy walked me out and lightly scolded me, like my grandparents used to do when I didn't eat at least two or more portions of the hearty meals they served. "Next time you have to come back with an ice chest to bring kielbasa home. Come prepared."

THE VICTOR CAFÉ

1303 DICKINSON ST. • PHILADELPHIA, PA 19147

(215) 468-3040 • VICTORCAFE.COM

A Serenade in South Philly

$\mathcal{M}$ usic like this is often performed in elegant surroundings complete with fancy chandeliers, showy private balconies, rich red plush seats, and gold-painted ceilings. It's performed in a venue that holds a few thousand people, where the talented artists wear lavish costumes.

At Victor Café, there are no private balconies nor rich red plush seats, nor gold-painted ceilings. The venue, two converted and joined townhouses, probably only holds a few hundred people at most. There are no lavish costumes either. Their "costumes" are plain white, complete with bow ties and aprons. There is a good reason for this: They're not costumes but uniforms. The opera singers are the waitstaff at the Victor Café.

This makes it even more shocking when you hear them sing, because the talented artists at Victor Café are just as talented as the ones I recently saw in that over-the-top venue described above, the Vienna Opera House in Austria.

The artists today are opera singers and often students training to be opera singers who come from schools like the Academy of Vocal Arts nearby in Philadelphia.

Originally, the singers were not the waitstaff but the patrons of Victor Café. What began as a gramophone shop in 1918 became the Victor Café in 1933. It was once a place to enjoy an espresso and listen to records with fellow enthusiasts, a place to have serious discussions about music until the early hours of the mornings. It then transformed into an Italian restaurant that often dually functioned as

188

a performance space. It was a place to sing, to eat, and, above all, to connect with other people who had a similar passion for music.

You'll understand this very quickly when you enter the Victor Café, where you will be overwhelmed by packed walls graced with old pictures of the hundreds of famous singers who have all enjoyed dinners and conversations, and often participated in singing sessions at the Victor Café. This includes people like Enrico Ernest Di Giuseppe, Luciano Pavarotti, Michael Crawford, and Tony Bennett. It also includes those lesser-known but just-as-special guests and customers, the ones who lived to hear and enjoy this music, spending their money on opera tickets above anything else. You'll find another few unexpected photos on the walls, like the one from the movie *Rocky Balboa*, filmed at the Victor Café in 2005. Sylvester Stallone and his crew spent weeks inside the restaurant filming, using it as the backdrop for the restaurant they called Adrian's. Some customers come in expecting it to be Adrian's. It's definitely not. That was fake. But those customers should not be disappointed when they see evidence of its real place in Philadelphia's history and experience the historical charm, lively atmosphere, and the booming voices that echo and reverberate through this restaurant every night.

John and Rose DiStefano were the ones who created this place. John had an immense knowledge of the music scene, especially in relation to classical music and the world of opera, and he got to know the executives at RCA Victor well, often chatting with and sometimes even informally advising them about talent. If you look up over the inside entrance, inside you'll notice a statue of the RCA's trademark image, Nipper the dog, head cocked, listening to a gramophone.

By the 1950s, after John DiStefano passed away, his two sons, Henry and Armond, kept the tradition going. Armond eventually left the business to share his love of music with others via a weekly radio show. Henry stayed involved, and today, the ownership of the Victor Café still remains within the DiStefano family as it has since 1918. Gregory DiStefano, Henry's son, is the current owner.

Decades ago the catchphrase "Music Lover's Rendezvous" was attached to the Victor Café. The neon sign still lights up the restaurant's exterior on this quiet, residential street in South Philly.

When you step inside today, you'll first experience the feel of a traditional Italian-style restaurant, with red-and-white checkered tablecloths and the smell of marinara sauce. You'll find welcoming Italian menu classics like cannelloni, a fresh pasta stuffed with spinach, veal, and ricotta. Choose from appetizers like baked clams casino, filled with minced clams, bell peppers, onions, bacon, and herbed bread crumbs, or their signature salad made with a Gorgonzola cheese dressing. Choose from meat dishes like veal saltimbocca stuffed with prosciutto, sage, and mushrooms. They're all great food options but still secondary to the primary reason you should visit.

It's for the moment when a brass bell rings, about every 20 minutes or so, and the waiters take turns sharing with you performances of songs that have created countless unforgettable moments for patrons of opera houses, Broadway theaters, and classical music venues around the world.

The opera industry is struggling today. Many opera houses in the US have closed in recent years, and some argue that opera's relevance in today's society is dying. Inside the Victor Café, they've found a way to keep it living, fighting on, and proving its relevancy.

Sandra, granddaughter of John DiStefano, who regularly still helps out in the restaurant's daily operation, confirms, "There's a living history going on here."

Appendix A

FEATURED PLACES BY CATEGORY

Bakeries

Cacia's Bakery, 13
Iannelli's Bakery, 99
Isgro Pasticceria, 103
Sarcone's Bakery, 162
Stock's Bakery, 177

Bars

Bob & Barbara's Lounge, 5
Bomb Bomb BBQ Grill & Italian Restaurant, 9
Cherry Street Tavern, 25
Cookie's Tavern, 33
Dirty Frank's Bar, 65
McGillin's Olde Ale House, 125
McMenamin's Tavern, 129
McNally's Tavern, 133
The Mermaid Inn, 136
Old Original Nick's Roast Beef, 139
Ray's Happy Birthday Bar, 159
Smokey Joe's, 169

Books

Joseph Fox Bookshop, 118

Butchers

Cappuccio's Meats, 20

Czerw's Polish Kielbasa, 45
Esposito's Meats, 69
Swiacki Meats, 184

Candy

Shane Confectionary, 165

Cheese

Di Bruno Bros., 56
Lucio Mancuso & Son, 122

Cheesesteaks

Campo's Deli, 17
Cosmi's Deli, 37
Dalessandro's Steaks and Hoagies, 49
Geno's Steaks, 87
Joe's Steaks & Soda Shop, 108
John's Roast Pork, 111
McNally's Tavern, 133
Pat's King of Steaks, 147

Clothing

Goldstein's Men's and Boys' Clothing, 91

Delis

Campo's Deli, 17
Cosmi's Deli, 37
Famous 4th Street Delicatessen, 72

Diners

The Dining Car, 60

Entertainment

The Mermaid Inn, 136

The Victor Café, 188

Fabrics

Fleishman Fabrics & Supplies, 79

Flags

Humphrys Flag Company, 95

Fruit and Produce

P&F Giordano, 143

Hoagies

Campo's Deli, 17
Cosmi's Deli, 37
Dalessandro's Steaks and Hoagies, 49
Joe's Steaks & Soda Shop, 108
John's Roast Pork, 111
McMenamin's Tavern, 129
McNally's Tavern, 133

Kielbasa

Czerw's Polish Kielbasa, 45
Swiacki Meats, 184

Kitchen Tools & Equipment

Fante's Kitchen Shop, 76

Ice Cream

Bassetts Ice Cream, 1
Joe's Steaks & Soda Shop, 108

Musical Instruments

Cunningham Piano Company, 41
Frederick W. Oster Fine Violins & Vintage Instruments, 82

Pasta (to prepare at home)

Di Bruno Bros., 56
Superior Pasta Company, 180

Restaurants

Bomb Bomb BBQ Grill & Italian Restaurant, 9
Cherry Street Tavern, 25
City Tavern Restaurant, 29
DeLuca's Villa di Roma, 53
The Dining Car, 60
Famous 4th Street Delicatessen, 72
McGillin's Olde Ale House, 125
McMenamin's Tavern, 129
McNally's Tavern, 133
Old Original Nick's Roast Beef, 139
Ralph's Italian Restaurant, 155
Smokey Joe's, 169
Snockey's Oyster and Crab House, 173
The Victor Café, 188

Roast Beef

Cherry Street Tavern, 25
John's Roast Pork, 111
McNally's Tavern, 133
Old Original Nick's Roast Beef, 139

Tomato Pies/Pizza

Cacia's Bakery, 13
Iannelli's Bakery, 99
Sarcone's Bakery, 162

Water Ice

John's Water Ice, 115
Pop's Water Ice, 151

Appendix B

FEATURED PLACES BY NEIGHBORHOOD

Center City

Logan Square

Cherry Street Tavern, 25

Market East

Bassetts Ice Cream, 1

Old City

Campo's Deli, 17
City Tavern Restaurant, 29
Humphrys Flag Company, 95
Shane Confectionary, 165

Rittenhouse Square

Joseph Fox Bookshop, 118

Washington Square West

Dirty Frank's Bar, 65
Frederick W. Oster Fine Violins & Vintage Instruments, 82
McGillin's Olde Ale House, 125

North

Kensington/Port Richmond

Stock's Bakery, 177

Port Richmond

Czerw's Polish Kielbasa, 45
Swiacki Meats, 184

Northeast

Tacony/Wissinoming

Joe's Steaks & Soda Shop, 108

Torresdale

The Dining Car, 60

Northwest

Chestnut Hill

McNally's Tavern, 133
The Mermaid Inn, 136

Germantown

Cunningham Piano Company, 41

Mount Airy

McMenamin's Tavern, 129

Roxborough

Dalessandro's Steaks and Hoagies, 49

South

Bella Vista

Cappuccio's Meats, 20
DeLuca's Villa di Roma, 53
Di Bruno Bros., 56
Esposito's Meats, 69
Fante's Kitchen Shop, 76
Goldstein's Men's and Boy's Clothing, 91
Isgro Pasticceria, 103

John's Water Ice, 115
P&F Giordano, 143
Ralph's Italian Restaurant, 155
Sarcone's Bakery, 162
Superior Pasta Company, 180

East Passyunk Crossing

Lucio Mancuso & Son, 122

Graduate Hospital

Bob & Barbara's Lounge, 5

Lower Moyamensing

Bomb Bomb BBQ Grill & Italian Restaurant, 9
Cookie's Tavern, 33
Pop's Water Ice, 151

Melrose

Cacia's Bakery, 13

Passyunk Square

Cosmi's Deli, 37
Geno's Steaks, 87
Iannelli's Bakery, 99
Pat's King of Steaks, 147
Ray's Happy Birthday Bar, 159
The Victor Café, 188

Pennsport

John's Roast Pork, 111

Queen Village

Famous 4th Street Delicatessen, 72
Fleishman Fabrics & Supplies, 79
Snockey's Oyster and Crab House, 173

West Passyunk

Old Original Nick's Roast Beef, 139

West

University City

Smokey Joe's, 169

Appendix C

FEATURED PLACES BY YEAR OF ORIGIN

1734: The Mermaid Inn*, 136

1773: City Tavern Restaurant*, 29

1860: McGillin's Olde Ale House, 125

1861: Bassetts Ice Cream, 1

1864: Humphrys Flag Company, 95

1891: Cunningham Piano Company, 41

1900: Ralph's Italian Restaurant, 155

1902: Goldstein's Men's and Boys' Clothing, 91

1904: Isgro Pasticceria, 103

1905: Cherry Street Tavern, 25

1906: Fante's Kitchen Shop, 76

1910: Iannelli's Bakery, 99

1911: Esposito's Meats, 69

1911: Shane Confectionary, 165

1912: Snockey's Oyster and Crab House, 173

1918: Sarcone's Bakery, 162

1918: The Victor Café, 188

1919: Stock's Bakery, 177

*Year specifies date that establishment originated. Denoted places have since been rebuilt or are replications of the original establishment.

1920: Cappuccio's Meats, 20

1921: McNally's Tavern, 133

1921: P&F Giordano, 143

1923: Famous 4th Street Delicatessen, 72

1930: John's Roast Pork, 111

1930: Pat's King of Steaks, 147

1932: Cosmi's Deli, 37

1932: Pop's Water Ice, 151

1933: Dirty Frank's Bar, 65

1933: Smokey Joe's, 169

1936: Bomb Bomb BBQ Grill & Italian Restaurant, 9

1936: Fleishman Fabrics & Supplies, 79

1938: Czerw's Polish Kielbasa, 45

1938: Old Original Nick's Roast Beef, 139

1938: Ray's Happy Birthday Bar, 159

1939: Di Bruno Bros., 56

1939: McMenamin's Tavern, 129

1940: Lucio Mancuso & Son, 122

1945: John's Water Ice, 115

1945: Superior Pasta Company, 180

1947: Campo's Deli, 17

1949: Joe's Steaks & Soda Shop, 108

1950: Cookie's Tavern, 33

1950: Swiacki Meats, 184

1951: Joseph Fox Bookshop, 118

1953: Cacia's Bakery, 13

1960: Dalessandro's Steaks and Hoagies, 49

1961: The Dining Car, 60

1963: DeLuca's Villa di Roma, 53

1966: Geno's Steaks, 87

1969: Bob & Barbara's Lounge, 5

1974: Frederick W. Oster Fine Violins & Vintage Instruments, 82

Photo Credits

All photos by Tanya Birch except the following:

Page 2: Courtesy of Bassetts Ice Cream
Page 16: Courtesy of Cacia's Bakery
Page 21: Courtesy of Domenick at Cappuccio's Meats
Page 46: Courtesy of Czerw's Polish Kielbasa
Page 61: Courtesy of The Dining Car

Bibliography

Keels, Thomas H., and Elizabeth Farmer Jarvis. *Chestnut Hill*. Charleston, SC: Arcadia Publishing, 2002.

Staib, Walter. *The City Tavern Cookbook, Recipes from the Birthplace of American Cuisine*. Philadelphia: Running Press Publishers, 2009.

Index

A

Anastasi Seafood, 174

B

barbecue, 9
Bassetts Ice Cream, 1
"Best Sandwich in America," 52
Betsy Ross House, 19, 96
Bicentennial, 30, 61
Bob & Barbara's Lounge, 5
Bomb Bomb BBQ Grill & Italian
    Restaurant, 9

C

Cacia's Bakery, 13
Campo's Deli, 17
Cannuli's Quality Meats &
    Poultry, 23
Cappuccio's Meats, 20
Cherry Street Tavern, 25
cigar shops, 171
City Hall, 2
City Tavern Restaurant, 29
Claudio Specialty Foods, 58
Cookie's Tavern, 33
Cosmi's Deli, 37
Cunningham Piano
    Company, 41
Czerw's Polish Kielbasa, 45

D

Dalessandro's Steaks and
    Hoagies, 49
Dante & Luigi's, Corona di
    Ferro, 158
DeLuca's Villa di Roma, 53
Di Bruno Bros., 56
diners, 62
DiNic's Pork & Beef, 52
Dining Car, The, 60
Dirty Frank's Bar, 65
drag show, 6

E

Enjay's Pizza, 170
Esposito's Meats, 69

F

Famous 4th Street Cookie
    Company, 74
Famous 4th Street
    Delicatessen, 72
Fante's Kitchen Shop, 76
Fiorella's Sausage, 23
First Continental Congress, 29
Fleishman Fabrics &
    Supplies, 79
Franklin Fountain, 167

Frederick W. Oster Fine Violins
    & Vintage Instruments, 82
Free Library of Philadelphia, 121
Freeman's Auction House,
    85, 167

G
Geno's Steaks, 87
Giovanni's Room, 120
Goldstein's Men's and Boys'
    Clothing, 91
Gracie, Charlie, 159
Grey Lodge Pub, 131
guitars, 84

H
Halloween, 67
Harry's Smoke Shop, 171
Humphrys Flag Company, 95

I
Iannelli's Bakery, 99
Independence Hall, 19
In Her Shoes (film), 73
Isgro Pasticceria, 103
Italian Market, 21, 53, 57, 69, 78,
    100, 143, 162, 182

J
jewelry store, 67
Jim's Steaks, 51
Joe's Steaks & Soda Shop, 108
John's Roast Pork, 111
John's Water Ice, 115
Joseph Fox Bookshop, 118

K
karaoke, 6
Koch's Deli, 75

L
Liberty Bell, 19
Lucio Mancuso & Son, 122

M
Marconi Plaza, 152
Marra's of Philadelphia, 101
Mayfair Diner, 62
McGillin's Olde Ale House, 125
McGlinchey's Bar, 7
McMenamin's Tavern, 129
McNally's Tavern, 133
Melrose Diner, 62
Mermaid Inn, The, 136
Mitchell & Ness Nostalgia
    Company, 93
Mummers, 66

N
National Constitution Center, 19

O
oldest family-owned Italian
    restaurant, 155
Old Original Nick's Roast
    Beef, 139
opera, 188

P
Pat's King of Steaks, 147
Pennsylvania Convention
    Center, 2
P&F Giordano, 143

Philadelphia (film), 73
Philadelphia Eagles, 93, 141
Philadelphia Flyers, 17
Philadelphia Phillies, 17, 141, 151
Philly AIDS Thrift @ Giovanni's
  Room, 120
pianos, 41
Pizza Olympics, 16
Pop's Water Ice, 151
Prohibition, 25, 133, 169

R
Ralph's Italian Restaurant, 155
Ray's Happy Birthday Bar, 159
RCA Victor, 190
Reading Terminal Market, 1, 52,
  74, 106
Rocky Balboa, 189

S
Saloon Restaurant, 158
Sarcone's Bakery, 162
Schmitter sandwich, 134
Shane Confectionary, 165
Smokey Joe's, 169

Snockey's Oyster and Crab
  House, 173
Staib, Walter, 29
Stock's Bakery, 177
Stoudts Brewing Company, 127
Superior Pasta Company, 180
Swiacki Meats, 184

T
Tacconelli's Pizzeria, 101
Termini Brothers Bakery, 106
Twin Smoke Shoppe, 171

U
University of Pennsylvania, 169
US Marine Corps, 33

V
Victor Café, The, 188
violins, 84

W
Washington, George, 30

Y
Yards Brewing Company, 31